T

WESTERN GEOPOLITICAL THOUGHT IN THE TWENTIETH CENTURY

Geoffrey Parker

CROOM HELM
London & Sydney

© 1985 Geoffrey Parker
Croom Helm Ltd, Provident House, Burrell Row,
Beckenham, Kent BR3 1AT
Croom Helm Australia Pty Ltd, First Floor,
139 King Street, Sydney, NSW 20001, Australia

British Library Cataloguing in Publication Data

Parker, Geoffrey, 1933-
    Western geopolitical thought in the twentieth
    century.
    1. Geography, Political—History—20th century
    I. Title
    320.1'2'091821   JC319
    ISBN 0-7099-2056-3

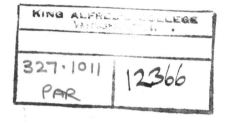
Typeset by Leaper & Gard Ltd. Bristol, England
Printed and bound in Great Britain
by Billing & Sons Limited, Worcester.

CONTENTS

FIGURES

To Martin and Julie

ACKNOWLEDGEMENTS

The author acknowledges the permission granted by the following for the reproduction of the copyright material as stated below:

Constable & Company	Figures 3.2 and 3.3
Hodder & Stoughton Educational	Figures 4.1, 4.2 and 4.3
Harrap Limited	Figures 5.1, 7.1, 8.4 and 8.5
Mrs Andreas Dorpalen	
Harcourt, Brace, Jovanovich, Inc.	Figures 7.2, 8.2 and 8.3
President Saul B. Cohen	Figures 9.1 and 9.2
Dr Arno Peters	Figure 10.1

PREFACE

In the first chapter of this book I have endeavoured to define geopolitics as I understand it. The term 'Western' is taken to comprise Central and Western Europe, together with North America. The central theme of the book is an examination of the thinking on this subject which has taken place in four particular countries, namely Great Britain, Germany, France, and the United States. They have been foremost in this field during the present century. Geopolitical terminology in English, French and German has normally been used without any specific explanation, but definitions of terms are to be found in the Glossary of Geopolitical Terms at the end of the book.

I acknowledge with gratitude the assistance which I have received from the libraries of the Royal Geographical Society and the University of Birmingham. Acknowledgement is specifically made to those authors and publishers who have kindly granted permission for their maps to be reproduced here. Finally, I take great pleasure in thanking my wife, Brenda, for her valuable and constructive advice, assistance and criticism throughout the writing of the book.

Geoffrey Parker

1 INTRODUCTION

Political and international power are complex and elusive phenomena and one must be wary of generalising too much about them. Thomas Carlyle's opinions on the nature and purposes of power had little in common with those of Karl Marx, while Lord Acton had different ideas from them both. What is evident is that its possession ultimately determines the international pecking order at any one time. It is the 'great powers' which have invariably been in the best position to influence the world situation in what they judge to be their own best interests. History, however, shows us that power is as ephemeral in a nation or empire as it is in an individual, its possession being no guarantee of its permanent retention. Inevitably it will slip away, and the reasons for this can be as difficult to explain as was its initial emergence.

Political geographers believe that power is firmly rooted in the physical nature of the world itself. Just as the giant Antaeus, offspring of Ge and Poseidon, the gods of Earth and Sea, drew his mighty strength from contact with the ground on which he stood, so the power of the modern state is derived from the territory which it occupies. If the earth were exactly round and polished like a billiard ball, said Jean Gottmann, then there could be no justification for such a study.[1] But the earth has great variety in climate, vegetation, soil, geology and altitude, together with an uneven distribution of the land masses, and these factors have made its surface into far more than merely the stage upon which the drama of human history has been enacted.

The terms 'political geography' and 'geopolitics', together with their respective adjectives 'politico-geographical' and 'geopolitical' have come to be widely used during the present century. However, the exact sense in which they are used is sometimes unclear, and there can be a danger of slipping into fine-sounding verbiage which is rather weak on precise meaning. What these terms do have in common is that they seek to identify an area of study which is concerned with the interface of geography and politics and with their mutual interactions. In some quarters the terms have come to be regarded as being virtually synonymous and at most as denoting degrees of emphasis. Distinctions, when they have been made, have often tended to take on an emotional or historical character. Thus by the middle of the present century 'geopolitics' had come to be closely identified with German *Geopolitik* which was tarnished by its association with the Nazis. Apart from this, the whole area of study was seen by many as being an actively propagandist version of the more scholarly 'political geography', and thus its claims to being an academic subject were often considered to be highly suspect.

In marked contrast to the persistence of such attitudes to 'geopolitics', the adjective 'geopolitical' has, in recent years, assumed considerable popularity with politicians, academics and journalists alike. Almost overnight, as it were, everything appeared to gain a 'geopolitical' dimension, this being understood in general terms to signify an awareness of the importance of geographical factors in human affairs. Mention of the term nowadays is calculated to conjure up visions of oil supplies, strategic minerals, agricultural potential, dangerous sea routes, vulnerable frontiers and, possibly, dwindling natural resources. It is no bad thing that the importance of geography has thus come to be implicitly recognised so widely, but more precision on the exact subject of the study becomes even more important.

In this book the term 'geopolitics', together with its adjective 'geopolitical', is defined as being the study of the international scene from a spatial or geocentric viewpoint, the understanding of the whole — what Ritter called *Ganzheit* — being its ultimate object and justification. An essential part of it is the examination of the components, but this is basically undertaken for the purpose of reaching a clearer understanding of the whole. Individual states can thus be seen as being the bricks, but it is the patterns and structures which they make in combination which are the principal interests of geopolitical investigation. Seen in this way geopolitics resembles climatology which seeks to understand global weather systems, while political geograhy is more analogous with meteorology which concentrates on the detail of local conditions in particular areas. The two are, of course, bound to be closely linked, but their objects and methods may be rather different. While the methodology of geopolitics is essentially spatial, its subject matter draws heavily on other social sciences. In view of this, the term is in many ways more appropriately considered as being itself a shortened form of 'geopolitical science'. Sir Peter Medawar's broad definition of science being 'the art of the soluble', the analysis and solution of world problems can certainly be regarded as being central to the purpose of geopolitical studies.[2] Through its emphasis on the importance of the understanding of the whole, it also possesses what Einstein called 'a feeling for the central order of things', and it has sought to achieve a better understanding of world political space both by analysis and by the postulation of hypotheses and theories. As East and Prescott saw it, the geopolitical world is 'a delicately interlocking mechanism'[3] and geopolitics is thus the study of how and to what end this 'mechanism' operates. Unlike the principal physical sciences, however, the method employed is that of synthesising the various elements which go into producing the totality so as to understand better the nature of the overall pattern.

Geopolitical thought has altered greatly during the course of the present century. It began at just that moment in history when the colouring of the polychromatic world political map was reaching its completion. The world dominance of Europe and the United States had become almost absolute and the territorial expression of this domination was the system of global empires covering a large portion of the earth's surface (Figure 1.1). Much of this territory had been acquired with considerable speed during the second half of the previous century, and its acquisition had been justified by recourse to such concepts as '*la mission civilatrice*', '*ein Platz in der Sonne*' and 'Manifest Destiny'. It was in this heady political climate that Halford Mackinder, often regarded as a founding father of modern political geography, produced his first great overview of the relationship of geography and history. Others had been thinking along similar lines, notably Friedrich Ratzel in Germany and the highly influential Alfred Mahan in the United States.

World War I was followed by major changes in this Western-dominated world order, and it also inaugurated a period of considerable international instability. Despite the fact that the German and Austrian Empires had been roundly defeated by the alliance led by Great Britain, France and, from 1917 on, the United States, the Congress of Versailles in 1919 failed to produce a lasting settlement. The European maritime empires began to show marked signs of weakening and the United States, now in economic terms the most powerful state in the world, retreated into voluntary isolation. Russia, re-emerging after the Bolshevik Revolution as the new Soviet Union, was forced into a similar, although largely involuntary, isolation. During the 1920s and 1930s right-

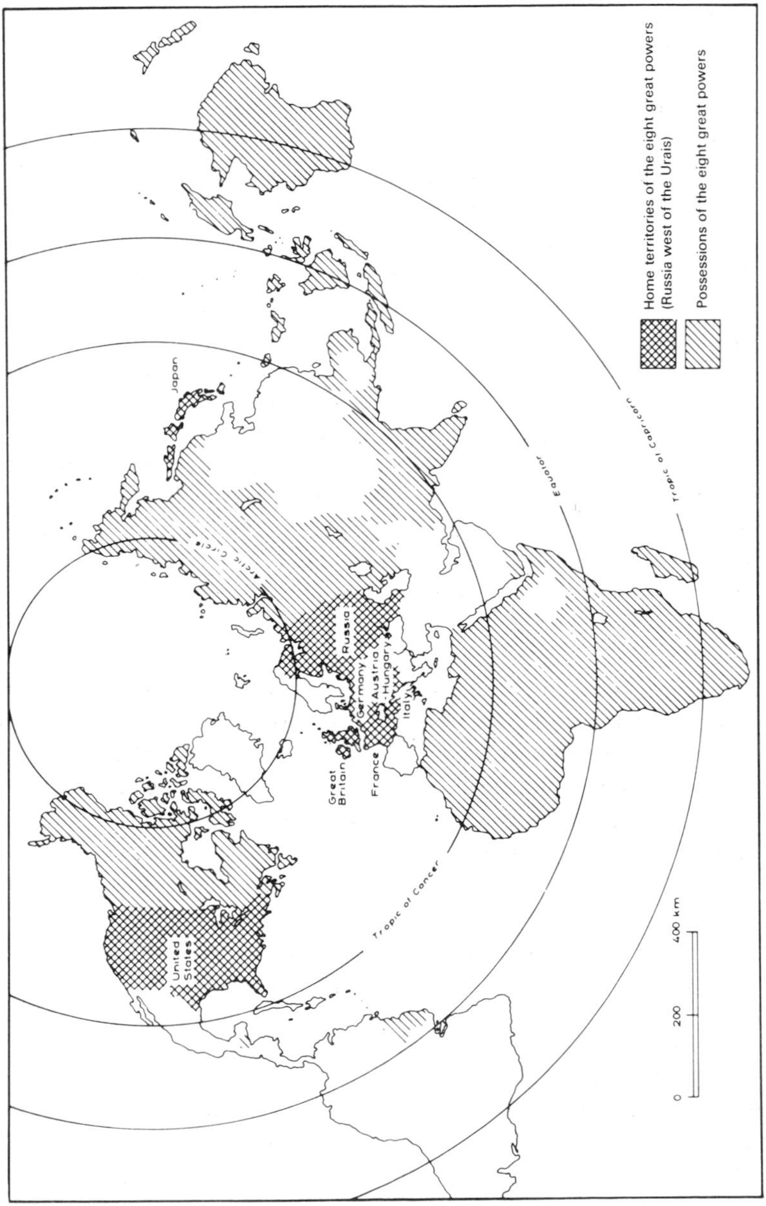

Figure 1.1: The Great Powers and their Possessions at the Beginning of the Twentieth Century

wing authoritarian regimes came into power in Italy, Germany and Japan which preached extreme nationalism and xenophobia. During the 1930s all three embarked on courses of territorial expansion which brought them inevitably into conflict with the maritime powers, in particular Britain and France. Much of the geopolitical thought of this period came to reflect this situation of conflict. It was the time when *Geopolitik* gained credence and prestige in Germany. This presented a distinctly German *Weltanschauung*, its object being to indicate a course of political and international action which would ensure a German victory in any future war. British and French geopolitical thinking was far less ruthless and single-minded, and indeed the prevailing geographical philosophy in France pointed towards alternatives of a far more civilised and peaceful kind. It was in the United States during the early years of World War II that the real challenge to German *Geopolitik* was mounted and a new geopolitics came into being. One of the principal objects of this was the creation of a distinctly American world view and a thoroughgoing examination of the country's world role. Following America's arrival at the centre of the stage in the aftermath of World War II, further geopolitical thinking sought to understand the cold war and the bipolar world, together with America's new position as one of the two superpowers.

In the early 1960s major changes began to take place on the international scene and the positions of both the superpowers showed some signs of slipping. In the new more fluid situation, political geographers entered into the debate on the development of more flexible approaches to world questions. This was followed in the 1970s by attention to issues such as world poverty, natural resources, the ecological balance and the ever more menacing nuclear threat in the age of Mutually Assured Destruction (MAD). Geopolitics, by its very nature eclectic and holistic in its approach, has been able to contribute to the debate on these and allied subjects of widespread concern.

Stephen Jones, recalling the mythical German scientist's voluminous and pedantic tome on the elephant, stressed that we must strive to see the whole animal even though at any one time we are likely to be able only barely and myopically to discern its outlines. He was convinced that, despite the pitfalls, 'the pursuit of the global view is the geographer's intellectual adventure'.[4] This book is principally an examination of those geopolitical thinkers who, during the course of the present century, have endeavoured to observe and interpret the whole. It will also suggest some ways in which both the thinkers and the thoughts may have had some influence on the course of events.

Notes

1. J. Gottmann, 'The Political Partitioning of Our World: An Attempt at Analysis', *World Politics*, IV, 4 (1952).
2. 'The Nature of Knowledge', *The Economist*, CCLXXXI, 7217-8 (1981).
3. W.G. East and J.R.V. Prescott, *Our Fragmented World* (Macmillan, London, 1975).
4. S.B. Jones, 'Global Strategic Views', *Geographical Review*, XXXXV, 4 (1955).

2 THE ROOTS OF TWENTIETH-CENTURY GEOPOLITICAL THOUGHT

Geopolitical thought in the Western world in the early years of the present century arose from the general intellectual and political atmosphere of the times. The *fin de siècle*, the end of the nineteenth century which had seen such tremendous advances in man's control of the physical world, was accompanied by a collective shudder of apprehension about the new century and what it might hold for mankind.

A number of very significant events heralded the arrival of the new century and these produced a widespread feeling that 'Victorian' stability was coming to an end and that a period of change was in the offing. The view inherited from the nineteenth century was of the world as a sort of pyramid with the Europeans, soon to be joined by the Americans, at the top and the 'uncivilised' natives inhabiting the other continents near the bottom. Europe's ruling classes, basing their authority on their control of the continent's land and capital, were at the very apex of this pyramid. Such a state of affairs, in all its social, economic, political and cultural manifestations, was deemed to derive its ultimate legitimacy from the Divine Will as communicated through the medium of the Christian churches. Particularly influential in the most advanced states was the Protestant version of Christianity which, through its encouragement of the work ethic, had presided over the progress of the Western world in the general direction of materialism. Europe was perceived as being the centre of the world, the source of the education and enlightenment of mankind and the principal location of his greatest triumphs. Europe was surrounded by an enormous and largely unknown swathe, consisting of most of the rest of the world, news of the exploration of which provided a constant diet of excitement for the masses. It was for the most part populated by dusky and 'uncivilised' races who supplied an exciting and romantic backdrop to the otherwise rather dull and prosaic commercialism of the European ascendancy. By the beginning of the twentieth century much of the dash and pageantry surrounding European imperialism derived from the colourful and mysterious cultures and environments of Africa and Asia.

7

Europe's pre-eminence amongst the continents of the world rested upon the techniques of exploitation which had been developed over the previous three centuries, while 'the white man's burden' consisted of the obligation to shed light into the world's dark corners and to wean their inhabitants away from their 'dark Egyptian night'. The advantages of the whole global enterprise to the European ruling classes were clearly enormous, while the benefits derived by the lower orders were less immediately apparent. For centuries their role had been that of hewers of the imperial wood and drawers of its water but now, in the more advanced West European countries at least, they were in course of persuading the rulers that it made good sense that they should be taken on as junior partners.

Well before the end of the century the foundations of this Christian, aristocratic and Eurocentric world order were being strongly undermined by a set of ideas deriving for the most part from the application of scientific thinking to social questions. Underlying it all was the scientific concept of a mechanistic universe controlled by blind impersonal forces which were the ultimate determinants of everything. More specifically, Darwin's theory of evolution had helped to start a major intellectual revolution which had torn like a cannonball through the conventional wisdoms of the late nineteenth century. In place of the Christian concept of a benevolent Creator breathing stability and permanence into his creation, thinking derived from Darwinism postulated constant change and evolution; endemic struggle replaced received order and, perhaps most momentous of all, man became essentially a part of the natural world rather than a being in the image of God. This particular Christian idea was replaced by the far less savoury spectre of man the ex-simian. The application of this thinking to human affairs was not long in coming. Herbert Spencer promulgated the idea of 'social Darwinism', a behaviourist philosophy maintaining that man's social activity was controlled by the same set of rules as those which applied in nature. Struggle was an essential component of human advance and 'the survival of the fittest' had determined the patterns of human social and political, as well as physical evolution.

Similar materialistic ideas were applied to human societies by Karl Marx who derived them for the most part from the German philosophers, in particular Hegel. For Marx the foundations of all societies were essentially economic, and consequently social advance was dependent upon economic change. This advance was brought by the tensions which developed within society as a result of the contradictions inherent in it. These contradictions eventually reached a stage in which they could only be resolved by the adoption of new forms of production and organisation. In this 'dialectical materialism' thesis and antithesis produced a new synthesis and it was in this way that progress took place. Thus as physical evolution had produced man at the top of the animal kingdom, so social evolution would eventually produce communism, the highest form of human organisation.

These and similar ideas for applying scientific thought to human activities came to constitute collectively an alternative to many aspects of the existing world order. States, churches, empires, monarchs, aristocrats and capitalists all found themselves under powerful moral, intellectual and even physical attack, and the possibility of the imminent collapse of at least some of them became a major cause of the *fin de siècle* malaise which had spread throughout Europe. The central problem both for the attackers and for those under attack was that of the most desirable order to replace the existing one, and there was, predictably, little agreement among them. Nationalists, anarchists, radicals, socialists and communists were among the many who ranged themselves against the established order, but each of them proposed a different solution. The power of their arguments, together with the violence which all too often accompanied them, shook but did not dislodge the European pyramid. Those at the top of the structure were well aware of the urgent necessity to give something of 'a place in the sun' to those people, classes, nations and states which considered themselves cheated by the prevailing distribution of social assets.

Thus to a certain extent the intellectual and scientific revolutions justified the most radical questioning of European social ideas, but in other, and arguably more profound ways, they paradoxically did much to reinforce the beliefs implicit in the European world view. The notion of the superiority of the white races over all others could now be justified and even reinforced by reference to the theory of evolution. As the human race owed its commanding world position to its superiority over the other animals, so the white race owed its superiority to this same process of evolution. It was argued that it was the struggle for existence and natural selection which had bred this hardy race of European mariners destined to dominate the world's lesser breeds. White could also, all too easily, be associated with enlightenment and goodness while black could be equated with darkness and savagery. It followed from all this that, whatever changes in social arrangements might ensue, Europe, in partnership with the United States, now possessed an armoury of new intellectual and philosophical weapons to justify her favoured position in the natural order of things.

The political geography of the twentieth century was thus born in a time of considerable political and intellectual turbulence. The specific form it took resulted from the effects of two particular stimuli. The first of these was the growing belief that major changes in society were inevitable and even desirable. The second was the widespread conviction shared by a growing number of students of the humanities of the importance of scientific, and particularly biological, theories in order to provide the explanation, rationalisation and direction of such changes. In turn this encouraged the belief in many quarters that the necessary changes could be accelerated by a collapse of the existing society brought about by a war involving the great powers. The old concept of the brotherhood of humanity was giving way to that of innate aggressiveness in the struggle for existence. As Ernest Lavisse gloomily put it in 1890: 'Today the most widespread of the systems of philosophy, that which has permeated the sciences, teaches of the necessity of the conflict for existence and the legitimacy of the selection made by the work of death.'[1]

Global geopolitical thinking at the turn of the century was also considerably helped by the fact that for the first time the potential subject-matter was at last revealed in something like its entirety. As Lord Bryce succinctly put it in his Romanes Lecture of 1902: 'The exploration of this earth is now all but finished. Civilised man knows his home in a sense in which he never knew it before.' He maintained that the features of the earth had 'passed from the chaos of conjecture to the cosmos of science' and concluded that 'the completion of this World-process is an especially great and fateful event'.[2] Two years later Spencer Wilkinson spoke more specifically of the international repercussions of this when he asserted that 'whereas only half a century ago statesmen played on a few squares of a chess-board of which the remainder was vacant, in the present day the world is an enclosed chess-board, and every movement of the statesmen must take account of all the squares on it'.[3] This closing of the world was certainly accompanied by a number of important occurrences on the international scene. The process of European imperial expansion, so frenetic in the last half of the nineteenth century, had begun to slow down and tensions were increasing over the apportionment of what remained. The European international order, based on an uneasy balance among the great powers, had now been projected into the other continents of the closed world. The history of Europe had now become that of the world.

The father of the new political geography was Friedrich Ratzel who was very much a product of German nineteenth-century thinking on philosophy and natural science. Geography and philosophy had been closely related in German academic studies since Kant, who had taken a particular interest in the physical environment and its effects on mankind and who saw all history as a kind of continuous geography. This engendered nineteenth-century holistic thinking in geography which was central to the spatial ideas of both Humboldt and Ritter. Ritter spoke of the unity of the organic whole as *Ganzheit* which was controlled by its own laws and was a manifestation of a teleological process.[4] To Humboldt the elements of the *Landschaft* repeated themselves in endless variations and he, like Ritter, saw order and purpose in the interrelationships of the whole. Ratzel was a part of this tradition of regarding the earth as an integral whole of which man was essentially a part. To be successful, it was necessary for man to adjust to his environment in the same way that the more successful flora and fauna had done. In his *Politische Geographie*[5] published in 1897 he followed the geopolitical implications of his thinking. It was Ratzel's contention that the state was a form of biological organism in a real rather than a metaphorical sense and that it behaved in accordance with biological laws. It also had a mind, something above and separate from those of the individuals who constituted its population, and it laboured under certain imperatives to ensure its continued existence. Furthermore, the state was to him a product of organic evolution, an organism attached to the land like a tree, and like a tree this 'space organism' had the roots of its being planted firmly in the soil. The characteristics of a state were therefore a consequence of the nature of its territory and its location and the measure of its success was contingent upon successful adaptation to these environmental conditions. It was natural and desirable for the healthy space organism to add to its strength through territorial expansionism.

Like Ritter before him, Ratzel was convinced that there were laws governing the relationships of the human and non-human phenomena on the surface of the earth and he expounded his own laws on the development of states. Successful expansion, he maintained, was not a simple territorial matter, but tended to occur in all fields simultaneously. The growing state will tend to absorb the less successful ones and will also aim to expand into what is strategically and economically the most valuable territory. While the impetus towards territorial expansion is likely to come initially from an external stimulus, it will go on to develop its own dynamism; in other words, the appetite for more territory comes with the eating of it. Every state needs to grow in this way if it is to flourish or it will decline and eventually disappear, incorporated into the territory of another more successful state. The whole process of the acquisition of *Lebensraum* not only makes the dynamic state more powerful but will make its people stronger and more enterprising and so fit to dominate ever larger territories.

Thus growth, struggle, evolution and decay, the ingredients of Darwinism, were present in the ideas of Ratzel. His main concern was with the process of change in spatial structures, as that of Marx was with change in social and economic structures. However, he never fully accepted natural selection nor the determinism which went hand in hand with it. Since the state, the organised political unit, in his view possessed its own mind, it also had some freedom of choice in the use of the potential afforded by the natural environment. He laid stress on the human will as a basic factor in the achievement of success as much by an organised group as by an individual.

Ratzel had considerable influence on the thinking of other political geographers at the beginning of the century. Rudolf Kjellén, the Swede who coined the term '*Geopolitik*', not only subscribed to the organic theory of the state, but pressed home the parallel characteristics of the organs of the state and those of the body (see Chapter 5). The capital city, centre of decision making, was the brain; the lines of communication were the arteries; the arms were defences and the physical resources were the food required for sustenance and growth. The state most amply endowed with these had the ability to become the most successful and to dominate the others.

Ratzel's ideas were taken to the United States by his devoted American disciple, Ellen Semple. Political geography was by no means new to America, however, since Arnold Guyot, 50 years earlier, had proposed a geographical pattern to the unfolding of world history. In the 1890s the influential Alfred Thayer Mahan, who was well known to the German geographers including Ratzel himself, had written at some length on the crucial importance of sea power in history[6] (see Chapter 4). Semple translated, interpreted and developed Ratzel's ideas in her *Influences of Geographic Environment.*[7] Following Ratzel, she emphasised not simply the inevitability but also the desirability of the territorial expansion of the dynamic state. Expansion has gone hand in hand with progress and as it has taken place so 'higher forms' have resulted. This she attributed to the fact that a widening of the geographical horizons has always produced 'the nutritious food of wide comparisons'. With Ratzel, she was of the opinion that the state had to expand into territory which would be of future value to it, but she also felt with her compatriot Mahan, that the control of the seas was another vital key to ensuring national success. Subsequently, however, Semple played down the organic theory of the state which to her and to other American geographers came increasingly to appear far-fetched. It must also be remembered that by the time Semple had introduced Ratzel's ideas to America the ties between biology and the social sciences had begun to loosen. Biological analogies were giving place to others, many of them now deriving from other sciences.

Many French geographers, and in particular the school of Vidal de la Blache, had also been very much taken with the concept of the 'earth organism' and of the unity of man and his environment. The idea of the earth as 'a living being in all its continuous variations' was implicit in the work of such geographers as Elisée Reclus and the all-embracing concept of *pays* contained and implied an almost mystical union of man with nature. However, French geographers were not happy about Ratzel's increasing concern with political matters and some saw it as part of that sinister German preoccupation with the state in the tradition of Fichte and Herder. To the French the real natural units were geograhical regions, not states, and geographers were considered as being more profitably engaged in the study of the former rather than the latter. Whilst they applauded Ratzel's comprehensive studies of human activities as part of the totality of the environment, they strongly objected to what Lucien Febvre called 'the monotonous chanting of old Ratzelian litanies'.[8] For them also the approach of the geographical determinists was 'sterile' and Vidal himself was of the conviction that geographers should resist the temptation to '*formuler les lois*', but rather should be concerned with interpreting the interplay of the variables which produce unique situations.[9]

In Germany, and in those countries which were strongly influenced by the German tradition, political geographers in the first decade of the twentieth century were concerned principally with the study of the spatial processes of the state and with the discovery of the 'laws' which they believed governed its behaviour. The importance and esteem of geography as an academic discipline in Britain at the time was far less than it was on the continent where it had an honoured position alongside history and philosophy. Nevertheless, it was in Britain that the most influential and all-embracing geopolitical outlook originated. To the country with by far the most significant involvement with the rest of the world, the completion of Bryce's 'world process' was of very special relevance. The concept of a global system to operate in the now closed world was to have a profound effect on all future geopolitical thought and it has become inextricably linked with the name of Sir Halford Mackinder.

Notes

1. E. Lavisse, *General View of the Political History of Europe* (Longmans Green, London, 1891).

2. J. Bryce, *The Relations of the Advanced and the Backward Races of Mankind*, Romanes Lecture (Clarendon, Oxford, 1902).

3. H.S. Wilkinson, 'Discussion Following the Presentation of "The Geographical Pivot of History" by H.J. Mackinder', *Geographical Journal*, 23 (1904).

4. R. Hartshorne, *The Nature of Geography. A Critical Survey of Current Thought in the Light of the Past* (Association of American Geographers, Lancaster, Pa., 1939).

5. F. Ratzel, *Politische Geographie* (Oldenbourg, Munich, 1897).

6. A.T. Mahan, *The Influence of Sea Power upon History* (Sampson Low, London, 1890).

7. E.C. Semple, *Influences of Geographic Environment* (Constable, London, 1914).

8. L. Febvre, *A Geographical Introduction to History* (Kegan Paul, London, 1932).

9. P. Vidal de la Blache, *Principles of Human Geography* (Constable, London, 1926).

3 HALFORD MACKINDER AND THE WORLD OUTLOOK

Prior to Mackinder there had already been a number of essays in the interpretation of the whole world situation from a spatial viewpoint. Many of these were ancillary to more general theories on the patterns of universal history. Both Hegel and Marx had been concerned with the development of systems of interpretation of universal history but neither was remarkable for depth of spatial perception, and for both of them the surface of the globe was largely a backdrop to historical events. Both, however, saw the European-Mediterranean region as the only area that really mattered in the world, the principal location of man's development, of 'progress' and the only place with a history worthy of the name. For Marx 'Eastern' and 'Asiatic' were terms synonymous with altogether lower levels of human attainment, having far more primitive social and economic systems. He refers to 'the temperate zone that is the mother country of capitalism', where, unimpeded by 'a too luxuriant nature', the physical conditions had stimulated the advance of mankind along its dialectically determined path.[1]

The main concern of political geographers, on the other hand, had been the description and interpretation of the state as a spatial phenomenon. While Ratzel had aimed at discovering the laws governing its development and the factors underlying its power, he also envisaged the eventual emergence of a pre-eminent world state. He was predisposed to think of this as being geographically European and racially Germanic and deriving its strength from the advantages of its territory. Across the Atlantic, Mahan enunciated the opposing view that it is the sea, 'the great highway', which has been the major factor in history, and the ultimate determinant of the wealth and strength of states.[2] The extent to which it is used in particular instances depends on location, physical configuration, territory, resources, population, national character and type of government. Mahan saw the control of the seas of the world as being in his time 'overwhelmingly in the West', a situation which had been emphasised by the events of the second half of the nineteenth century. In Mahan's view Britain was the only nation so

15

well endowed with the factors of power as to be capable of attaining world supremacy. His main concern in his historical survey of sea power had been to show how important it was for the United States to seize the opportunities which lay within her grasp and to become herself a major maritime and colonial power. As Strausz-Hupé put it, 'a lusty imperialism lent wings to Mahan's imagination ... and opened in the 1890s new horizons to the revivalists of Manifest Destiny'.[3] Mahan reached almost mystical heights in his encouragement to his compatriots to seize the Philippines: '*Deus vult.* It was the cry of the crusader and the Puritan and I doubt if a man utters a nobler.' His realisation of the crucial role of sea power was, according to Barbara Tuchman, 'one of those perceptions that turn inward darkness into light'.[4] His ideas were duly noted in Berlin and they became influential in helping to justify the Kaiser's naval policy and in helping to mould subsequent German attitudes towards Britain. The Kaiser now became even more convinced than ever that Germany must take to the water, and according to one writer the works of Mahan 'must have seemed almost like a divinely inspired signpost along the road to glory'.[5]

It was Halford Mackinder, however, who drew these various strands of thought together to produce what L.S. Amery called 'a comprehensive idea'. This was first put forward in 1904 as 'The Geographical Pivot of History'[6] and was subsequently developed and modified in 1919 in *Democratic Ideals and Reality.*[7] The former was therefore produced shortly after the end of the Boer War and the latter during the immediate aftermath of World War I. The 1904 paper was seminal although there are clear indications in earlier works that he had been thinking along these lines for some time. Hartshorne later called it 'a thesis of world power analysis and prognosis which for better or worse has become the most famous contribution of modern geography to man's view of his political world'.[8] At the beginning of the twentieth century Mackinder considered that the time was ripe for such an analysis since the world had become 'a closed political system' and at the same time what he called the 'Columbian epoch' was, after 400 years, coming to its end. European history had become world history and the repercussions of events would from then on be felt everywhere, like stones cast into a pond. He therefore concluded that '[We] are for the first time in a position to attempt, with some degree of completeness, a correlation between the larger geographical and the larger historical generalisations' and so to embark upon an examination of 'geographical causation in universal history'.

Mackinder's central thesis in 1904 was that world history was basically a recurring conflict between the landsmen and the seamen. The most powerful centre of land power, he maintained, had always been the heart of Eurasia and it was from there that 'the great Asiatic hammer' had steadily struck outwards into the maritime fringes. This central heart of Eurasia is an enormous area consisting largely of steppe and desert land, surrounded by mountains on most sides and with interior or Arctic drainage. It is thus a gigantic natural fortress, largely inaccessible to the seamen, but as a result of the harshness of the natural conditions it has in the past been able to support only a sparse and mostly nomadic population. Around the southern and western fringes of Eurasia is a great crescent in which the physical conditions have been far more favourable to the development of human societies. This is the domain of the seamen and it consists of four separate populous areas — China, India, Europe and the Middle East. The latter area has been historically the weak link through which the landsmen have been able to penetrate into the maritime crescent. It was essentially this threat and pressure from the east which had stimulated the exceptional development of European maritime activity. This began the Columbian epoch in the 'Tudor century' when the Europeans rapidly expanded over the insular and peninsular lands and so were able to create new Europes out of the reach of land power. At about the same time the Russians turned the tables on the Mongol steppemen and embarked on the conquest of Siberia. Since then they had been in course of organising that vast area and it had developed into a more formidable source of power than ever it was in the hands of the nomads themselves.

Here Mackinder came to the main thesis of his world view. The centre of the Eurasian landmass, that remote region of interior and Arctic drainage was, he believed, 'the pivot of the world's politics'. In it Russian domination had now replaced that of the nomadic empires, and this had placed that country in an immensely strong international position (Figure 3.1).

The marginal lands of the world consisted of two concentric crescents. There was the inner or marginal crescent which had nurtured the great historic civilisations of Europe, the Middle East, India and China. Then there was the outer or insular crescent made up of the Americas, sub-Saharan Africa and Australasia.

Figure 3.1: The Geographical Pivot of History

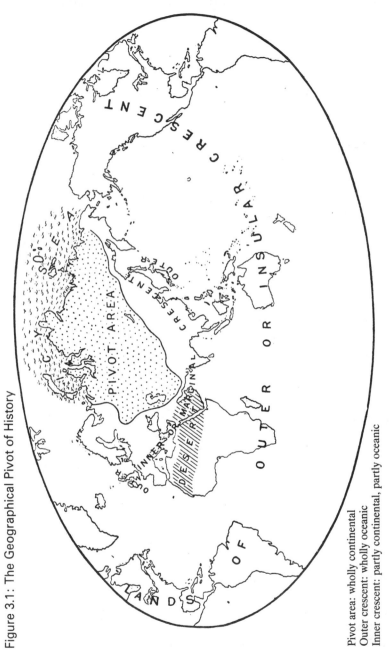

Pivot area: wholly continental
Outer crescent: wholly oceanic
Inner crescent: partly continental, partly oceanic

Source: Mackinder, H.J., The Royal Geographical Society, *The Geographical Pivot of History* (GJ, London, 1904).

Although Britain was undeniably a part of Europe, its insularity from the continent put it in effect into the outer crescent. The major international issues of the early twentieth century, particularly those of the Near East and the Far East, were, in his view, the result of the state of unstable equilibrium existing between the pivot and the inner crescent in these regions.

The conclusion of the thesis was that while during the Columbian epoch sea power had been superior to land power, at the beginning of the post-Columbian epoch the balance of advantage was beginning to tip in favour of the land. The maritime mobility which for centuries had been the greatest asset of the seamen was now being challenged by continental mobility brought about by the development of the railways. Thanks to the contiguity of the central landmass, the pivot state when organised was ideally placed to probe the margins and to expand into them. If it proved to be successful in doing this, then the maritime states could be dislodged from their peripheral toe-holds and 'the empire of the world would be in sight'. While Russia was the obvious candidate for the role of pivot state, it was nevertheless conceivable to Mackinder that other continental powers could now pursue pivot policies and this might accelerate the whole process. As early as 1890 Mackinder had speculated that 'it may be that the balance of geographical advantages has already inclined against England, and that she is maintaining her position by inertia'.[9] The message, loud and clear, was that it was imperative for the maritime world, led by Britain, to gird its loins against the coming dangers. It was also in the interest of the maritime states, with France in the role of continental bridgehead, to ally together and to attempt to wean Germany away from any temptation to engage in a pivot policy. Underlying the whole 1904 paper is a note of fear and apprehension that in the post-Columbian epoch the maritime world was already on the defensive and that the future lay with land power. It followed from Mackinder's interpretation of history that the pivot state would prevail unless countervailing action were taken with some urgency.

Mackinder's second major essay in the formulation of a comprehensive world outlook, *Democratic Ideals and Reality*, was written some 15 years later during the winter which followed the end of World War I. It too is permeated by a feeling of urgency, this time arising from the writer's strong conviction of the need to capitalise on the victory and to secure the most advantageous possible peace. Mackinder felt that time was of the essence and that new international structures should now be established without delay. The opportunity afforded by the war to embark upon this task should not be missed. As he saw it, young societies can be moulded like soft clay whereas when they get older they become fixed and firm. This applied to the fluidity of the international situation at the time which was likely soon to harden off.

The fundamental thesis of the dichotomy of land and sea power remained central but there were significant changes in both form and content and a new expressive terminology was introduced. Europe, Asia and Africa now became the 'World-Island', the landmass with by far the largest area and population and the principal stage of world history. While its northern coasts were barren and movement along them was impeded by the Arctic ice, those to the south and west were navigable throughout the year. These coasts, stretching from Europe around Africa to the Indian Ocean and beyond together constitued the 'World-Promontory' which since the sixteenth century had been controlled by the seamen from Europe. The great maritime crescent around the coasts of the promontory had in this way achieved a certain unity, particularly in communications and commerce. Associated closely with this crescent was 'the North American sea base' regarded as being not so much a continent as a kind of off-shore island of the World-Island itself. The 'Pivot' was now renamed the 'Heartland', and its relationship to the European section of the maritime crescent was seen as being closer than that with the rest of it. The reason for this was the existence of the 'great lowland' (Figure 3.2) stretching across Eurasia and encouraging the landsmen to move in a generally westerly direction. The particular character of European civilisation arose from this steady pounding by the land power 'as between pestle and mortar'.

Mackinder now proposed two extensions of the Heartland from the Pivot of 1904. One of these was into the mountainous regions of central Asia which were hardly accessible to sea power although the drainage was for the most part to the ocean (Figure 3.3). The other, and by far the most significant, was the inclusion of the drainage basins of the Black Sea and the Baltic, thus encompassing Eastern Europe as far as a line from the Elbe to the Adriatic. When land power was strong, the Black Sea and the Baltic were virtually inland seas and access could be denied to maritime power. Mackinder then went one step further and pronounced that

Figure 3.2: The Great Lowland of Eurasia

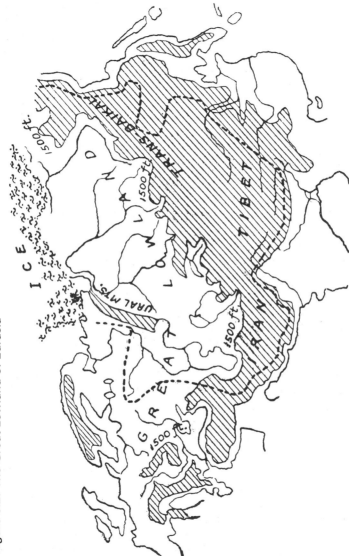

Source: Mackinder, H.J., *Democratic Ideals and Reality* (Constable and Company Ltd, London, 1919).

the possession of Eastern Europe is the key to the control of the Heartland. This thesis was encapsulated in the famous triptych whispered to the assembled world statesmen by his 'airy cherub':

Who rules East Europe commands the Heartland:
Who rules the Heartland commands the World-Island:
Who rules the World-Island commands the world.

The incorporation of East Europe was a significant development in Mackinder's thinking and clearly stemmed from what had happened in the world since the beginning of the century. Germany, or Prussia as Mackinder still liked to refer to it, had definitively replaced Russia in his mind as the principal danger to the security of Great Britain. Since the late nineteenth century 'the centre of gravity in East Europe was being shifted from Petrograd

Figure 3.3: The Heartland

Source: Mackinder, H.J., *Democratic Ideals and Reality* (Constable and Company Ltd, London, 1919)

to Berlin' but this fact and its importance had not been fully appreciated. It was the historical antagonism between German and Slav arising from the former's persistent drive to control East Europe which was now seen as having been the principal cause of the World War. This German *Drang nach Osten* inevitably drew her towards the Heartland and thus towards the possibility of replacing Russia as the principal power throughout the region. Already in 1904 Mackinder had referred to Russia as a 'tenant' of the Heartland and had speculated on the possibility of her eventual replacement by other powers. This did not at the time alter the thesis in any fundamental way since whichever power did control the Heartland would operate under the same geographical constraints as did Russia herself; in other words it would be forced by its circumstances to behave in much the same manner as the latter. The sinister development since then was that Germany had become sufficiently powerful, efficient and motivated to achieve such control and so to take the historical process to its doom-laden conclusion. The use of the name 'Prussia' was now doubly significant since this implied the association of Germany with the warrior state on the eastern marchlands, the historic core of which lay well within the enlarged Heartland. On the other hand Germany did belong to both the western and eastern parts of Europe, and it had been her failure to choose between 'Hamburg and overseas dominion or Baghdad and the Heartland' which inevitably led to the great blunder of war on two fronts. It was without doubt 'Junker militarism' which had triumphed and had erected a 'Rhenish glacis' to protect it in the west. Despite its defeat, this ascendancy of the organisation of Berlin over the idealism of Frankfurt boded ill for the future.

Mackinder then came to World War I itself, in the aftermath of which he was writing. In essentials, in his opinion, it had fitted into the historical patterns which he had outlined in 1904. It was in essence a war between seamen and landsmen fought mainly on the landward front of peninsular France. The collapse of Russia and the entry of America into the war in 1917 had cleared the view of reality and 'purified our ideals'. For a short period Germany, in pursuance of her pivot policy, had been able to control much of Eastern Europe and Russia, but in the end land power was defeated and sea power was again in the ascendant. This situation would, prima facie at least, have appeared to be a vindication of Mahan's optimism, but Mackinder was not easily taken in by outward appearances. He refused to deviate substantially from his contention that, despite its massive setback, the balance of advantage was still on the side of land power. This was attributable to its strategic invulnerability, territorial contiguity and massive physical resources. These were increasingly being drawn together by a network of railways and potentially dominated by a race of organisers. The Heartland would become the centre of world power when it was possessed by 'a garrison sufficient both in number and quality'. The war had not in any way altered these basic elements in the situation. In addition to all these advantages, there was also the new factor of air power which in Mackinder's estimation was another arm of land power. It was a new 'amphibious cavalry' capable of interfering with maritime communications in such vital but highly vulnerable places as the Mediterranean-Red Sea routeway.

It followed from these arguments that while Germany and Russia were in 1919 both prostrate, they would certainly recover and be subjected once more to some form of autocratic rule and ruthless organisation. Either together or apart they would then once more constitute a menace to the maritime nations. Such developments would nurture that 'single World Empire' the coming of which Mackinder saw and dreaded and which it was his main aim to try to prevent.

The final development in Mackinder's 1919 thinking was on the question of the international future. It was more essential than ever that the warlike tendencies inherent in states had now to be curbed. He saw the fundamental cause of war as being the unequal distribution of the world's resources and its strategic potential. It was necessary now to make states come to terms with the geographical circumstances of their own existence. This was the 'reality' which they had to accept and to live with. Idealism was the desire to promote more positive and fruitful relationships among states, but it ignored reality at its peril. The existing order of things always arose out of the nature of the geographical conditions. This is what he called the 'going concern' and it was the necessary foundation of a secure and lasting future. It would be the height of folly to attempt to destroy it for the sake of implementing quite unproven ideals. If it were to have any chance of success, the new League of Nations had to take account of existing realities and to build upon them. It should be the aim to produce a real balance of the states of the world so as to ensure that not one of them became sufficiently powerful to be able to challenge it. It was the dominance of one member which had made such federations as the German Empire merely a pretence, while the United States and Switzerland, having no such predominant partner, had been far more successful. One way of attempting to ensure such a balance in the international arena would be to institute some form of 'trusteeship' by the great powers which would act in concert to ensure that the principles of the League were upheld. An Anglo-American maritime trusteeship would be a powerful guarantee for the security of the world's seaways. Another possibility which he put forward was that of federations of smaller states so as to give them collectively some of that balancing strength which individually they clearly lacked. Eastern Europe, at long last fully liberated from the tyranny of the continental powers, was a region in which some such international federalism might usefully be attempted. It would have the added advantages of discouraging any German ambition to renew her expansion to the east and of strengthening the 'third tier' between Germany and Russia. Such a removal of the temptation to conquest through the achievement of a balance of force would also be a considerable encouragement to good neighbourliness. In Mackinder's opinion the alternative to the search for effective international structures would be a return to a world in which force was the final arbiter and conquest always the goal of the aggressor state. If this were to happen, men would have no alternative to the role of being 'slaves to the world's geography'. Such determinism was now rejected as the only possible future, and mankind was put firmly into the driving seat. 'Today we realise, as we emerge from our fiery trial, that human victory consists in our rising superior to such mere fatalism.'

Mackinder's world outlook, which had been substantially modified between 1904 and 1919 was later to be fundamentally revised in his final 1943 paper, 'The Round World and the Winning of the Peace'.[10] This was, of course, produced in very different circumstances from those of the first quarter of the century and it, together with later criticisms of the Heartland theory, are discussed in Chapter 8. While Mackinder's thinking on world issues clearly evolved between the first decade of the twentieth century and the period of World War I, certain features remained fairly constant. From the beginning it was holistic, founded on the proposition that the totality of global phenomena contained a spatial process which rewarded examination and was susceptible to rational interpretation. The morphology of the process resulted from the interaction of the human dynamic with the relative stasis of the non-human environment. The formation of Mackinder's world outlook dates from the late nineteenth century and like that of most of his contemporaries it was influenced by the Darwinism of the time. He was himself originally trained as a biologist and he shared the belief then common amongst human geographers in the close relationship between their subject and the physical sciences. Biological terms appear a great deal in his works and there is also an underlying concept of the organic character of geopolitical phenomena, of struggle for existence and the survival of the fittest. While close to Ratzel in his concept of the state as organic, he never subscribed to the latter's search for biological laws. Human geography was not for him a nomothetic subject since the processes he studied occurred only once and they were produced by a large number of variable factors operating in unique circumstances. His use of biological terms may therefore often have been for the purposes of analogy since this was a favoured mode of expression in the social sciences at the time.

Associated with this approach, however, is the implied determinism in the use of such terms as 'inevitable', 'control', 'govern' and 'compelling destiny'. In the 1904 paper this is spelt out in the phrase 'man and not nature initiates, but nature in large measure controls'. This is certainly nearer to Ratzelian ways of thinking than to the possibilism of the French school. Again in 1919 the statements of the 'airy cherub' appear quite deterministic about cause and effect on the path to world domination. From the use of such terminology one can only conclude that the larger geopolitical processes at least were considered as being determined. Already in 1890 he had talked of 'the ways in which geographical features govern or, at least, guide history' and of 'how deep are the ruts in which a nation's course is run'. In the 'world organism' of the 1904 paper it is the environment which has shaped the broad outlines of the human dynamic and also produced its consequences. It is also in the nature of the process that the advantage lay at the time with land power in seeking to 'command the world'.

From the maritime viewpoint it is a profoundly gloomy *Weltanschauung* and this was precisely what Mackinder intended it to be. The key to its understanding lies in the statement that while this is how the process has operated in the past and, on the basis of the evidence, may continue to do so in the future, it does

not absolutely have to be this way. It is this which makes his determinism, after all, conditional. What he is saying is that things will
go on happening in this way only if we let them so happen. Mankind does have the capacity to rise above the world historical
process, or rather to have some influence on the direction in which
it goes. In practical terms this meant that the British Empire could
be saved from the historical fate of previous empires, but only by a
conscious effort of will. Before World War I this had entailed for
him the replacement of the ease and self-satisfaction of the
Edwardian high summer by something like the sort of dynamism
and efficiency which he saw in Germany. Only by taking the
historical process by the ear, so to speak, could Britain be saved
from the fate prescribed for her by the new balance of advantage.
For Mackinder it was only possible through, and in full knowledge
of, the realities of the contemporary world situation. In the wake of
World War I his emphasis changed to that of reliance on the
collective strength of the maritime world as a whole so as to maintain the ascendancy which, temporarily in Mackinder's view, it had
once again achieved. In the new circumstances the British Empire
had to seek its salvation in alliance with America and the other
maritime states; in other words the alliance system of the second
half of World War I had to be perpetuated into the years of peace.

This and all the rest of what Mackinder was now advocating
presupposed a high degree of potential for emancipation from
those environmental bonds which had historically been drawn so
tight. The 'mere fatalism' implicit in Darwinian theory is now
replaced by an optimism arising from the possibility of 'human
victory' over the dictates of the environment. Despite this, the
geographical environment, the world system, still remained the
ultimate reality, the 'going concern'. To imagine that it could now
be ignored was 'cant' and it would certainly take its revenge. Man's
victory had to be brought about through the environment rather
than from it, and in this context it is significant that the infant
League of Nations was described as being 'the landscape gardener
of civilisation'. All the subsequent thinking was set firmly on the
proposition that it was imperative for mankind, the 'psychosphere',
to co-operate with the world as it was if man was to be a successful
agent in its future course.

Mackinder's geopolitical outlook, then, arose from an analytic
and interpretive examination of the world historical process.
Adopting the spatial viewpoint it was an attempt to probe to the

essence, to the 'why' of events, and through a synthesis of all the
elements involved to achieve a coherency which had not until then
been attained. He also sought to use his particular insights in order
to extrapolate the likely future course of events. He always maintained that his world outlook was intended as a philosophical basis,
a kind of intellectual blueprint, for urgent action by Britain and her
allies. It was without doubt born of the fears felt by him and others
for the future of his country at the end of that Columbian epoch
during which it had attained to so splendid but so dangerous a pre-
eminence.

Although the subsequent influence of Mackinder's ideas on
western geopolitical thought has been enormous, their impact at
the time would appear to have been surprisingly small. This was
despite the fact that, as Blouet saw it, the Heartland theme was
deeply rooted in British imperial experience and its florescence
was very much a product of the age (see Chapter 8). In addition to
this Mackinder was an active public figure at the time. He knew
and worked with political leaders such as Joseph Chamberlain and
Lord Rosebury and gave considerable support to the Liberal
Imperialists and tariff reformers. He played a prominent part in the
political and social debates of the time and was a follower of the
contemporary vogue for 'political economy'. He was a founder
member of the 'Coefficients Club' established by the Webbs in
1902, other members of which included Bertrand Russell, Leo
Amery, Alfred Milner and H.G. Wells. Like many 'top people' of
the time, the members of this group were acutely aware of the very
real symptoms of national decline in Britain, and their self-
appointed task was to bring about a reversal of this situation.
Amery later called it 'a Brains Trust or General Staff',[11] while to
Wells it was about 'What are we doing and what are we going to
do with the world?'[12] Whatever their political views, they all felt
that there was need for a new 'efficiency' to replace the Edwardian
self-satisfaction. It was in this context that Mackinder first used
such terms as 'going concern' and 'manpower'. Initially a supporter
of the Liberal Party, he left to join the Conservatives and was a
Member of Parliament from 1910 to 1922. He had been very
active while at Oxford, disseminating his ideas widely through
extension lectures given in many towns throughout England. Subsequently he was involved in the establishment of the University of
Reading and of the London School of Economics of which he was
to become Director.

In 1919 Lord Curzon, then Foreign Secretary, appointed him to the position of High Commissioner in Southern Russia. In the wake of the Bolshevik Revolution, the situation there was chaotic and Mackinder was required to report back on it to the British government. In this position he was inevitably closely involved with the development of British policy towards the Bolsheviks. Mackinder's world view was now fully developed and it led him to be extremely fearful of the impact of these events on the British Empire. He was clearly attracted by the idea of detaching the non-Russian nationalities, such as the Ukrainians, from the new Soviet state giving them independence within an extended eastern buffer zone. This was to prove impractical in view of the amount of support which the Bolsheviks commanded, although the three Baltic states, along with Finland and Poland, did gain their independence and a wide buffer zone was created.

Democratic Ideals and Reality was thus the product of the thinking of an active man of affairs and not of a solitary recluse in the groves of academe. It was always Mackinder's intention that his geopolitical ideas should be an aid to statecraft and should assist in the enlightenment of those, often holders of high office, who were ignorant of the geographical realities of the world. Yet there is little evidence that many of the political leaders of the time were aware of, let alone understood, what he was trying to say to them. During the discussion following Mackinder's 1904 paper Spencer Wilkinson remarked that he 'looked with regret on some of the space that is unoccupied here', and regretted too that 'a portion of it was not occupied by members of the Cabinet'. The same sentiments might have been applied to the Cabinet of 1919 with the outstanding exception of Lord Curzon himself. Mackinder did not generally make a very favourable impression on the House of Commons. His vision of the world seemed to practical men of affairs to lack relevance, and the Left thought of him as being an imperialist. At the Congress of Versailles in 1919 and at the other peace conferences of the time the political leaders were preoccupied with the solution of the immediate problems which faced them. Most of them appeared to have had little time for the longer-term implications of their decisions or for putting them into the wider context of geography and history. It appears that their collective geographical knowledge was often sadly lacking and there are many instances of confusion arising from ignorance of the facts,[13] ignorance of a kind which Bowman subsequently attempted to rectify in *The New World*[14] (see Chapter 7).

As for the British people as a whole, there was certainly an abundance of idealism in the wake of World War I, and this focused on the notion that it had been 'a war to end wars' and would be followed by a perpetual peace guaranteed by the new League of Nations. In other sections of the population there was a predisposition towards a more brutally realistic approach, much of it of a 'make Germany pay' and 'hang the Kaiser' variety. The central intellectual problem was that idealism and realism were rarely blended in the subtle manner which Mackinder saw as being essential to the successful resolution of the issues facing the world.

Among the other major victorious powers the United States was most idealist and France most realist, and there was an international failure to bring the two together. President Woodrow Wilson had enunciated his 'Fourteen Points' as war aims, and embarked on a crusade to make the world safe for democracy. Clemenceau, commenting acidly that '*le Bon Dieu*' had made do with only ten, embarked on a policy of ensuring the permanent security of France through maintaining the permanent weakness of Germany. Following Congressional rejection of the Treaty of Versailles and the defeat of Wilson in 1920, the United States withdrew across the Atlantic and began a period of isolationism which was to last for nearly 20 years. France, destined by her geography to a deep and permanent involvement in the affairs of continental Europe, pursued her aims with an often savage realism. But the spirit of Clemenceau was to prove more vengeful than realistic and the new European system created at Versailles was to last barely two decades. Mackinder's geopolitical ideas can have had little influence in France at this time since his 1919 book was not translated into French, nor even reviewed in *Annales de Géographie*. Across the Atlantic it was Admiral Mahan who had been the greatest influence on the American devotees of *Realpolitik*, and his ideas were to become important again in the 1930s as the United States began once more to edge towards the centre of the international stage.

While Mackinder was the first geographer to attempt a truly comprehensive world view, linking geography and history in one broad canvas, there can be few more telling examples of the truth of the saying that a prophet is often least honoured in his own country. Hans Weigert expressed the opinion that the 1904 paper, delivered at a time when Britain was still widely thought of as being at the height of her world power, 'seemed shocking and fantastic to many in the English-speaking world'.[15] Besides, the English were traditionally suspicious of large ideas, tending to leave them to the less pragmatic foreigners. It was in the country of the defeated enemy that the ideas which Mackinder had intended as a guide for his fellow countrymen were shortly to be taken up with interest and incorporated into a formidable central European *Weltanschauung*. It was to take a quarter of a century and another world war to bring Mackinder to the serious attention of Anglo-Saxon geographers and political leaders.

Notes

1. Quoted in M. Quaini, *Geography and Marxism* (Blackwell, Oxford, 1982).

2. A.T. Mahan, *The Influence of Sea Power upon History* (Sampson Low, London, 1890).

3. R. Strausz-Hupé, *Geopolitics: The Struggle for Space and Power* (Putnam, New York, 1942), Chapter 17.

4. B. Tuchman, *The Proud Tower* (Hamish Hamilton, London, 1966), Chapter 3.

5. T 124, *Sea Power* (Jonathan Cape, London, 1940).

6. H.J. Mackinder, 'The Geographical Pivot of History', *Geographical Journal*, 23 (1904).

7. H.J. Mackinder, *Democratic Ideals and Reality: A Study in the Politics of Reconstruction* (Constable, London, 1919).

8. R. Hartshorne, 'Political Geography' in P.E. James and C.F. Jones (eds.), *American Geography: Inventory and Prospect* (Association of American Geographers, Syracuse, NY, 1954).

9. H.J. Mackinder, 'The Physical Basis of Political Geography', *Scottish Geographical Magazine*, 6 (1890).

10. H.J. Mackinder, 'The Round World and the Winning of the Peace', *Foreign Affairs*, XXI, 4 (1943).

11. G.R. Searle, *The Quest for National Efficiency* (Oxford University Press, Oxford, 1971).

12. H.G. Wells, *Experiment in Autobiography*, Volume 2 (Gollancz, London, 1934).

13. E.J. Dillon, *The Inside Story of the Peace Conference* (Hutchinson, London, 1919).

14. I. Bowman, *The New World*, 3rd edn. (Harrap, London, 1926).

15. H.W. Weigert, *Generals and Geographers: The Twilight of Geopolitics* (Oxford University Press, New York, 1942).

4 GLOBAL VIEWS AFTER MACKINDER'S PIVOT THEORY

During the period between the publication of 'The Geographical Pivot of History' in 1904 and the years immediately following World War I there were a number of other important contributions to the development of a global outlook appropriate to the age of the closed world system. They came principally from geographers and political thinkers working in Britain, Germany, the United States and France, and while their concepts were often very different, they were all influenced by the ideas of Mahan, Ratzel and Mackinder.

First off the mark was Leo Amery who took the opportunity of the discussion immediately following the delivery of Mackinder's 1904 paper to put forward an alternative world view.[1] Amery was of the opinion that Mackinder had overstated the importance of the 'Pivot' as the future centre of world power, and that this view was not borne out either by its history or its geography. As an alternative to Mackinder's view of history as having been the confrontation of two world systems based respectively on the sea and on the land, he proposed his own three — the interior steppe, the marginal agrarian and the maritime coastal. The strongest of these in economic, demographic and territorial terms had been the marginal agrarian and this had supported the principal centres of civilisation since early times. Both the steppe and the maritime systems possessed less physical power, but they had the advantage of being able to retreat to the safety of their continental or maritime homelands which were for most of the time out of reach of marginal power. At periods when the marginal civilisations had been weak, as a result either of economic difficulties or of political divisions, the landsmen or the seamen had been able to dominate them. In this way Asiatic nomads, such as the Mongols and the Turks, had been able to establish vast empires in the Middle East and Eastern Europe, and seamen such as the Vikings and the Elizabethan English, operating from restricted bases, had been able to prevail against much more powerful continental states. During the nineteenth century a fourth system — the industrial — had been added to the three others, and it was Amery's contention that this was

32

likely to become the most important of all in the future. He concluded that 'the successful powers will be those who have the
greatest industrial basis ... and the power of invention and of
science'. He also foresaw that in the future air power would introduce an entirely new strategic element into the situation. In this he
was remarkably prescient since the pioneering flight of the Wright
brothers had taken place only in the previous year, and Mackinder
appeared not to have thought much of its implications at the time.
States had normally achieved pre-eminent power through control
of more than one of the four systems, and Amery saw Britain as
being both a maritime and an industrial power. The Japanese
Empire, then rising in the east, also owed its strength to the same
two systems. All the maritime powers in his view needed to combine together in order to counteract the Pivot, 'to act upon the
marginal region, maintaining the balance of power there as against
the expansive internal forces'. Thus in the end, like Mackinder,
Amery saw danger emanating from the Pivot, but he saw the real
strength in industry and science, out of which combination the new
air power would emerge.

Lord Curzon, viewing the world more pragmatically from the
perspective of the Viceregal Lodge at Simla, was disposed to see it
as the stage on which Britain played out her world destiny of
bestowing the advantages of her rule on as large a part of it as
possible. His principal concern in *Frontiers*[2] was with the continued security of the ever more vulnerable imperial limits, in
particular those of the Indian empire, and with their maintenance
by a vigorous forward policy. The European empires, with Britain
in the vanguard, were deemed to be the legitimate inheritors of the
decaying empires of Eurasia. The frontier was seen as being the
key to successful empire and to the maintenance of the imperial
will in the nation: 'Along a thousand miles of remote border are to
be found our twentieth century Marcher Lords.' Whether the full
implications of the historical comparison were fully appreciated by
Curzon is not clear, but he certainly used his geographical thinking
to justify a muscular and if necessary expansionist foreign policy.

British imperial interest in the marginal lands of Eurasia was far
less welcome to Joseph Partsch of the University of Breslau. In his
Central Europe[3] he conjured up the spectre of a world dominated
by two gigantic powers, intending this as a dire warning to the
German people of what could happen if *Mitteleuropa* were not
united and strong. He talked of the former 'chimera' of Europe's

becoming one day half Jacobin and half Cossack being replaced by the equally undesirable prospect of its being divided between 'the colossal empires of Great Britain and Russia'. These two were now in a position between them to subjugate the marginal lands. While his attitude to Great Britain appeared to be the then traditional German one of envy tinged with admiration, there is clearly a very real apprehension of 'the Russian colossus in its unceasing expansion' and of *Mitteleuropa* at some future time disappearing from view into 'the maw of the monster'. Breslau is clearly a very different vantage point on the world scene from Simla, and most of the conclusions drawn from it were different. However, Partsch did share the apprehension of Curzon and other British geographers as to the likely future course of what Lavisse had referred to as 'the Russian glacier ... always sliding onward'.[4] Presciently Partsch foresaw that the future balance of the twin world colossi would need to be maintained by 'the development of the United States and by the vast population of Eastern Asia'.

A very different world perspective from the European continent was provided by Vidal de la Blache writing before and during World War I.[5] Like the others, he was well aware of the dichotomy of the maritime and continental worlds, but he envisaged the former as prevailing over the latter. The unity of the world's seas and the unequalled ease of communication which they facilitate was the greatest advantage which the seamen possessed. Through the exploitation of this the creation of the empire of the seas — 'Oceana' as he called it, after Froude[6] — had become a possibility for the British thalassocracy. This was the first example of power on a truly global scale and he saw this thalassocracy as moving from the coasts and into the interiors of adjacent continents: 'The peripheral zone is widening. The sphere of influence of the sea is spreading in the interior.' The British Empire has thus become a continental as well as a maritime power: 'Delhi has just replaced Calcutta as capital of India; what began as a customs house has become an empire.'[7] It was through this increasing extent of the province of the sea that world unity appeared to Vidal to be most likely. For him, as for Western geographers generally, this would have the unquestioned advantage of being founded upon the methods and values of the maritime world. Closer to Mahan than to early Mackinder, Vidal's brief excursion into internationalism nevertheless produced thoughts which were not dissimilar to the solutions proposed in *Democratic Ideals and Reality.*

The British geographer James Fairgrieve interpreted the entwined geography and history of the world in a far more comprehensive manner than any other of the period except Mackinder himself. Although his *Geography and World Power*[8] was first published in 1915, it was in fact written mainly before the war had begun. The development of Fairgrieve's thought is reflected in the subsequent editions of his work which went on into the 1930s. Like Mackinder, Fairgrieve's approach is historical and he traces world history from the spatial viewpoint from early times to the twentieth century. The distribution of the land area of the world was fundamental in this and he saw its centre as being 'the old world parallelogram' (Figure 4.1) cut diagonally in two by a belt of low-lying and submerged land. This belt was the principal centre of the history of mankind, and it was from here that the coasts of the parallelogram were subdued and brought into the world maritime system dominated by Europe. He used the terms 'heartland' and 'great plain of the world' for the centre of Eurasia, the home of the pastoral nomads. He postulated an intermediate crush zone which was the meeting place of the maritime and continental worlds (Figure 4.2). This had the advantage of being linked with both the sea and the land and it gained strength from this. In post-war editions of his book Fairgrieve followed Mackinder more closely in seeing the importance of this zone as linked to the future role of Germany when she had recovered from defeat. He perceived the dual personality of Germany: 'In touch with the sea and tempted on to the ocean [she] is one of the sea powers, while her position on the western and most populous margin of the great heartland makes her, at any rate, a possible centre from which that heartland might be organised.'[9]

Fairgrieve saw the principal purpose running through the ebb and flow of history as being the continuous aim of mankind to produce and control energy more effectively. Since this energy had to be produced from the physical environment, that environment determined the direction and success of the search, and so history became a product of geography. Energy is present in many different forms and the exploitation of them is conditional upon man's technical advance. The attacks by the aggressive nomadic societies of Eurasia upon the agricultural lands of the margins have throughout history been motivated by the necessity of augmenting their own limited supplies of energy. The most important aspect of the Industrial Revolution was that it increased the supply of avail-

Figure 4.1: The Old World Parallelogram

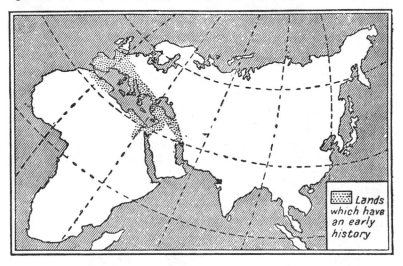

Source: Fairgrieve, J., *Geography and World Power* (University of London Press, London, 1932).

able energy through the harnessing of the power contained in coal. The principal source of the world's coal, and so of energy, was a great belt stretching from west to east across Europe and picked up in similar strata across the Atlantic.[10] This had become also the centre of the world's industry. The possession of energy was therefore in his view a major attribute of international power in the modern world.

Fairgrieve then examined the dominant position achieved by the world's temperate lands, and in particular by Europe. This he saw as having been a consequence of the relatively difficult and challenging life which the climatic conditions imposed upon their inhabitants. It related also to the accumulation of surplus energy since the conditions promoted 'the mental stimulus ... towards saving energy in the so-called temperate regions'. These regions were therefore associated with human 'advance' and 'strength', while in the less challenging tropics there had been 'a lack of virility'. He considered this to be the basic environmental explanation for 'the advance of Europe and the darkness of the Dark Continent'.[11]

Fairgrieve then went on to consider the implications of the similar climatic conditions to be found throughout the whole of the

Figure 4.2: The Old World System

Centres from which the Heartland has been dominated: the Altai, the Turan, Russia.

Centres from which the Heartland might be dominated: Germany, China, India.

Lands of the Sea Powers.

The Crush Zone.

The Heartland.

Source: As in Figure 4.1.

temperate lands of the northern hemisphere. He considered the 'Northern Belt of Settlement and Movement' to have contained 'the lands that mattered' in history (Figure 4.3). 'The history of the world', as he saw it, 'is mainly the history of temperate regions lying roughly between latitudes 30° and 60° N' and the most energetic of mankind were north of 35°. The great centres of the world's civilisation lay in Europe, India, the Far East and North America and were linked together by a chain of communications, 'a continuous circular service' by sea and land. The older sea routes had been complemented by transcontinental rail communications creating a kind of global axial belt: 'New York and Montreal, Vancouver and San Francisco, equally with Tokio, Nagasaki, Omsk, Moscow, Shanghai, Colombo, Alexandria, Berlin, Paris and London are seen to lie on these main routes by sea and land and air.' There was of course a climatic belt having similar conditions south of the Equator, but the land areas there were too small and discontinuous, and they were relegated to the role of relatively unimportant fringes of the northern centres of power.

In addition to the provision of terrestrial and climatic energy, there is further the historical significance of the sea as a provider of protection for the maritime peoples against those of the continent. Fairgrieve contended that 'a sea power can be crushed only by a sea power' and that seamen will always defeat landsmen on the seas. Thus in this respect he was aligned with those who believed that the sea could prevail so long as the seamen used their advantages prudently. They had the energy and the power which derived from its possession, and they had the potential strength to repulse attack from the land. Their security could be achieved by the unity of the countries of the maritime world inspired and led by Britain. Britain, France, Italy, Portugal, and Japan together held 'all the lands girdling Euro-Asia' and together they had the ability to control the tropical lands and box in the heartland.

After World War I Fairgrieve saw the establishment of some sort of world organisation as the answer to the problem of securing international peace through equilibrium. Both he and Mackinder envisaged this organisation as controlled by the Western powers and institutionalising a world order which would be in their best interests. However, while Mackinder thought of the League of Nations as the great international 'landscape gardener', to Fairgrieve it was a mechanism for global energy-saving, the busi-

Figure 4.3: The Northern Belt of Settlement and Movement

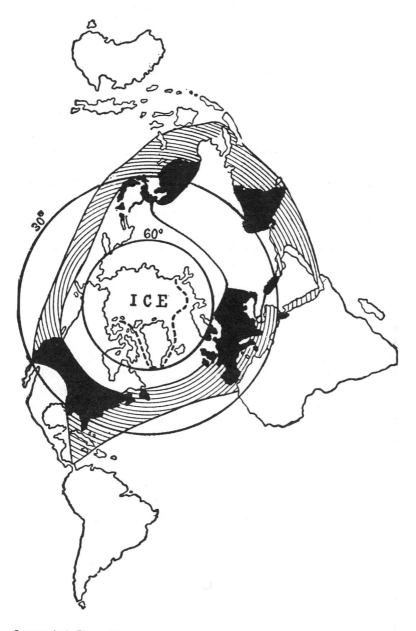

Source: As in Figure 4.1.

ness of which would be to ensure that valuable energy resources would never be so wantonly frittered away again. In the end Fairgrieve always returned to the question of energy which was to him the central resource most vital to man's future. At that time coal was dominant, but he saw it as being limited and finite and it was necessary to consider the situation when supplies had become exhausted. He proposed wind, water and oil, although the latter did not at the time appear to loom very large in his thinking. It was the sun itself that he saw as being the greatest potential source of energy, and this was most available in the tropics and in particular in the hot deserts where insolation was at its highest. All this suggested to him 'changes in the relative importance of areas' and a new significance for the tropical regions of the world if their climatic disadvantages, which had made them so unattractive in the past, could be overcome with the aid of modern science.[12]

A final political geographer of this particular period was Vaughan Cornish, who wrote in the years immediately after World War I. He saw the centres of power in the modern world as having grown up in the temperate zone and especially in the lands bordering the North Atlantic where the 'two principal foci' of occidental civilisation lay around the great coalfields. He was one of those who saw the balance of advantage as having swung away from the maritime world and consequently the position of Britain as the pre-eminent maritime power as having slipped. *A Geography of Imperial Defence*[13] was written with the same kind of urgency which Mackinder had displayed three years earlier and, like Mackinder, he foresaw grave dangers to the Empire in the emerging world situation. His answer to this was the encouragement of the balanced development of a 'Confederate Empire' which would take into partnership the other Britains beyond the seas. The Empire would be made stronger by this spread of wealth and power, and so be able to withstand more easily the centrifugal forces which were coming to operate within it.

Each of the political geographers discussed above had his individual *Weltanschauung*, but certain themes are common throughout the thinking of this period. Most basic was the acknowledgement that the world could now be viewed as a whole for the first time. The age of virtually unlimited expansion at the frontiers of the known was approaching its end and was being replaced by a closed and finite system with very different implications for international relationships. From then on what happened in one part of the world, like the ripples from a stone thrown into a pool, was going to affect everywhere else, and it was vital that the great powers should rapidly learn how to live in the situation of limited space. The unity of the planet implied, in a way never conceived of before, the unity of humanity in what Semple had called 'an inseparable whole'. At the beginning of the century the nature of this terrestrial unity was conceived of mainly in biological terms. It was an organic whole, and, at the most extreme, it was believed to function in a quasi-biological manner. Geopolitically, it was composed of organic units, the states, which were themselves analogous to living beings and were subject to the laws of nature, experiencing growth, development and decay and feeling 'hunger' for more territory. The more extreme protagonists of the organic theory took these qualities literally, considering that the state really was a living body. Others used these organic terms more loosely, more by way of analogy with the kind of processes they wished to suggest and explain. The term 'heartland' is, of course, itself a coupling of the biological and the terrestrial in one evocative term, but the links in this case were never pressed to any conclusion.

Inextricably linked with the organic theory and following on from it was the Darwinian idea of struggle, of the eventual survival of only the fittest political organisms. Struggle was an inherent feature of the life of states as it was with animals, and was the mechanism whereby the selection procedure operated. This concept of struggle was positively welcomed by some as an important concomitant of the activity of the dynamic state. Curzon, who otherwise was happy to welcome what he saw as encouraging signs of the development of internationalism in the years before World War I, also saw the opportunities afforded by the powerful expanding state for promoting virility in its people, and as the 'best university' for the young. Semple, following Ratzel, regarded the acquisition of territory as wholly desirable and a fundamental factor in progress. This was Semple's 'law of increasing territorial aggregates' in which intellectual force was liberated by that 'nutritious food' which came from expanding geographical horizons.[14] The conclusion of such thinking was that the strong would quite literally inherit the earth and, like Antaeus, draw more strength from its plenitude. Expansion was thus *ipso facto* a desirable thing. Another concomitant of the belief in the biological process was environmental determinism. While there was widespread agreement on the importance of environmental influences, there was disagreement and even ambivalence as to the exact extent of these. Words such as 'control', 'result', 'determine', 'natural', 'law' and 'inevitable' appear frequently in the geopolitical writings of the time. Such terms assert that man's activities are the consequence of the operation of the elements of the terrestrial system and that he is powerless to escape them. As Fairgrieve put it, 'geographical conditions have in a very real if somewhat general sense controlled history'. Such actual or implied determinism is found alongside the use of terms suggesting that man, while 'influenced' by the environment, has nevertheless a certain choice in the matter. There is once more ambivalence, such as Fairgrieve's comment that Germany was 'naturally forced or tempted' to pursue a certain course, while at the same time he accords greater freedom to France 'deliberately choosing to look landward rather than seaward'.[15] This ambivalence underlies the polemics of political geography at the time, in which a frequently doom-laden scenario is depicted, and then ways are suggested for ensuring that it is not translated into reality. The Titanic may after all be able to avoid collision with the iceberg if remedial action is speedily taken on the bridge. Thus the possibility of choice must be conceded if blind destiny is not to make any advice proffered totally meaningless and pointless. The apparent contradiction of attempting to avoid the inevitable can also be looked at from the standpoint of attempting to change the nature of the quasi-biological processes. Just because the process had historically operated in a certain manner and in accordance with certain causative factors, it did not necessarily follow that it was bound to be the same in the future. The possibility of change being brought about by the free operation of the human will could not be discounted. The problem here was that in the geopolitical world outlook mankind did not and could not possess that free will which was a fundamental attribute of mankind in the Christian world outlook. He was a part of a quasi-organic world process the functioning of which was dependent upon a large number of terrestrial variables. The contention was that if he tried to extricate himself and attempted to exercise total free will then not only would he have no influence on the course of events, but could even destroy himself. Thus if his individual actions were to have meaning it had to be as part of the process and as an agent in steering its future course. Man's actions were constrained by the total environment which itself even influenced his mental attitudes; as Fairgrieve put it: 'Geographical controls produce their effects by acting upon the minds of men.' This belief is a fundamental component of Mackinder's 'reality', the totality which must be accepted as the basis for all action, the 'going concern' which has been produced by the momentum of history. It is within and through this reality that the will must be used to generate positive action to move the whole in the desired direction.

Inherent in the idea of the developing world process was the assumption of progress, that great Victorian belief that things were advancing onward and upward, and that the millenium would eventually be reached through man's mastery of the physical world. As Fairgrieve said: 'History is not all repetition, there has been an advance.' He goes on to suggest, with more than a tinge of embarrassment, that through 'the orderly relation of events' some 'increasing purpose runs'. He later even hazards the suggestion that 'though the mills of God grind slowly, they grind exceedingly small' — one of the few intimations of Divine participation in modern political geography. To Fairgrieve the mills of God were likely to be most effective when they were most efficient in their use of energy. Associated with the assumptions underlying material advance there had been a strong feeling before World War I that progress was taking place in international relations. An element of general progress was the feeling that civilised mankind was at long last learning to live without war. This would enable the world system to develop and improve without being shattered as in the past by the eruption of the stresses and strains within it. War just did not make any sense any more for the great industrial powers of the world, and Fairgrieve saw it in quite clinical terms as a stupid waste of energy, to be avoided on these grounds alone. To Semple international organisation appeared as the natural outcome of that historical process which led towards the expansion of the relations between the civilised peoples of the world. 'Are we in process of evolving a social idea vaster than that underlying nationality?' she asked, and partly answered her own question with another: 'Do the Socialists hint to us the geographic basis of this new development when they describe themselves as an international political party?'[16] Partsch also occasionally displayed a certain underlying optimism in spite of all his foreboding about the future of Europe. He discerned a 'growing enlightenment' which he ascribed to the rather prosaic fact that peace was the first condition for successful labour. However, alongside this basic optimism on the subject of international relations, there was clearly a marked strain of pessimism running through the thoughts of many British geographers of the period. This appeared to arise from the perception of the way in which geopolitical analysis led to the inescapable conclusion that the world position of Britain was beginning to slip. It is this more than anything else which seems to have been responsible for engendering the idea that man himself can become a positive agent of change in the world system and move the process out of those historical 'ruts' which in 1904 had appeared to Mackinder to be so deep.

The great advance of mankind, the progress which it was confidently assumed had been made over the centuries, was ascribed in large part to the productive interplay of two natural phenomena, the sea and the climate. The seas of the world were viewed by almost all the political geographers of this time as having been a fundamental factor in human progress. The general advance and enlightenment of mankind was seen as having been accomplished by the sea peoples dwelling around the rim of Eurasia. At his best, man was to these geographers virtually an aquatic animal, or at least an amphibian which on land became slow and ponderous. Semple saw the sea as beckoning mankind, while to Fairgrieve it was creative in contrast to the continent which was destructive and cruel. To him the sea had been the 'controlling influence' historically and the thalassic states had been in the vanguard of mankind.

The second phenomenon was climate, and there was general acceptance of the proposition that the temperate belt of the Northern Hemisphere had played a particularly important part in the advance of mankind. 'The North Temperate Zone is preeminently the culture zone of the earth', said Semple, and she attributed this to the fact that the environment 'exacts a tribute of labour'. Here 'nature has given much by withholding much. Here man found his birthright, the privilege of struggle.'[17] Like Marx before him, Fairgrieve made the general assertion that these were 'the lands that mattered', and the only ones with a history worthy of the name. Ellsworth Huntington was at this time studying the effects of climate on civilisation, and he ascribed the leading position of the temperate belt to the cyclonic control which acts as such a stimulant to human activity within it. Europe retained its dominant position and 'wherever one turns, he feels the tentacles of the great European center of civilisation reaching out and vivifying the life of the whole world'.[18] Outside Europe he saw the United States as being the only country 'which has succeeded in touching the daily life of the world as a whole'.

It was in Europe that these two phenomena were seen to have come together most fruitfully and to have produced the highest civilisation on the planet. There appear to have been few doubts as to the superiority of the Europeans as is indicated through the use of such terms as 'civilised peoples', 'civilised powers', 'higher civilisation', 'advanced peoples' and even 'the peoples that matter'. The whole thing was even defended by 'civilised armies', but there was only qualified praise for the methods which these latter employed. The conquest of the globe by these 'virile people' was consequently seen as being both natural and desirable, and it went without saying that it was also to the advantage of the 'uncivilised' or 'barbarous' to succumb to the beneficient influences of civilisation. This all led naturally to a fundamentally Eurocentric, or at least Occidocentric, view of the world. Fairgrieve refers to the 'outlying areas' being brought increasingly into the world system. Already there was a disposition to perceive through the divisive, polychromatic imperialism of the day, a maritime Europe which had the potential for some form of unity. There is also the disposition to see such unity as desirable, even urgent, so that the civilisation of the seamen could be strong enough to resist the dangers which would come, as they always had, from the continent. Strongly implied in all this was also the organic idea of Europe as being the brain of humanity which had the moral right and duty to organise the rest of mankind as it saw fit.

To conclude, there were in the early twentieth century a number of basic assumptions in geopolitical thinking which were rarely questioned. There was the belief that the interacting phenomena on the surface of the globe were susceptible to holistic interpretation and explanation; that they all knitted together to produce a meaningful spatial pattern; that this pattern was not a fixed one but was in process of improvement through gradual change and modification. No longer was much attention given to the notion of a Divine Plan after the manner of Ritter. Yet, rather than being jettisoned, the Christian God had in effect been incorporated and metamorphosed into a sort of mechanistic spirit presiding over material progress. Belief in a quasi-organic social system gave rise to a quasi-religious materialistic system based on the virtues of strength, virility and power and assuming the superiority of those societies which possessed them. The metaphysical and the physical came together in that muscular Christianity which sought to justify the aggressive spirit in terms of an earlier and gentler belief. Great vision could be engendered by the perception of great space and moral good could flow from hitching the pioneer's wagon — or an army's munition train — to a star. The expansion of the civilised peoples over the surface of the earth was a natural concomitant to this and could thus be nothing but desirable. It was the evolutionary social process which had put Britain and the rest of the maritime world in the forefront of mankind. Yet there were now apparent dangers from the continuation of the process and these needed to be counteracted by decisive action, bringing the human will to bear on changing the course of destiny.

World War I changed the world scene dramatically and it shattered the great illusion that the powers of the civilised world had lost their taste for war or their belief that force was the ultimate arbiter of human affairs. It also destroyed the belief in gradual progressive social evolution. Europe in particular had been overtaken by a catastrophe of massive dimensions, and nothing could ever be looked at in quite the same way again. Yet the effects of this trauma are less immediately apparent in the writings of political geographers in the immediate post-war period. This is because the maritime world had superficially changed far less than the marginal and continental states. The Western powers had after all triumphed, while the continental powers were in chaos, and this appeared to vindicate those who had been confident of the fundamental strength and resilience of the maritime world. The basic causes underlying the pessimism of the pre-war years thus seemed to have been removed and 'Oceana' was triumphant. The concept of an international order as institutionalised in the League of Nations was in effect directed towards the consolidation and perpetuation of this state of affairs.

All this had profound implications for the world process viewed geopolitically. It was in effect an attempt to slow the process down, to stop it even, and in particular to deflect it from the menacing course foretold by Mackinder and others. Darwinian evolution was thus quietly toppled from the central position which it had up to then held. This was partly because as an explanatory system it had not matched up to the catastrophic realities of that appalling war. Far from being explicable in Darwinian terms, it appeared to represent a regression to a darker and more terrible period of man's history. In addition — and this had been apparent well before the war — Darwinism was ceasing to be an acceptable part of the presiding ideology of an Europe, and more particularly a Britain, which was losing its pre-eminent position in the world. In Victorian times evolutionary change had implied progress, but this was no longer necessarily the case. From being the philosophical underpinning of material progress, development and advance, such change began to take on the appearance of a drift into decline and fall. The notion of the impending 'death' of Europe was a final organic analogy which was far less acceptable than had been those earlier ones associated with vitality and growth.

In this way evolution, so congenial a philosophy in the expanding world of the nineteenth century, came to be replaced by a kind of neo-creationism in the closed and less friendly world of the twentieth. The aim, whether conscious or not, of those political geographers who wrote in the aftermath of World War I was to demonstrate how the world process could be arrested and frozen at a moment in history particularly favourable to the interests of the maritime powers.

By the time of World War I Lord Curzon, one of the writers discussed in this chapter, was very much at the centre of world events. In 1916 he was appointed to Lloyd George's War Cabinet and in 1919 he became Foreign Secretary, a position he was to hold until 1924. His fundamental international attitudes had changed very little since his years as Viceroy of India and he remained a missionary protagonist of empire, convinced that India was still the key to Britain's pre-eminent position in the world. This, together with his privileged aristocratic background, goes some way towards explaining his political credo and the policies which he founded on it. Yet he was also a geographer and, however grandiose his imperial vision, it was well rooted in geographical reality. He had always been scornful of those diplomats who had drawn remote frontiers 'in the happy irresponsibility of their official chairs'.[19] To him artificial frontiers were highly dangerous and this particularly applied to Britain which, besides being the world's greatest maritime power, was also now the greatest land power. Britain's vulnerable position could best be secured by a policy of developing spheres of influence and buffer zones within which disputes could more easily be contained and resolved. At the various peace conferences Curzon was a major protagonist of this approach which came to be the policy followed by the Western powers. Strausz-Hupé attributed this to Curzon's influence, stating that 'the shape of Europe as it finally emerged from the Council rooms of Versailles, Trianon and St Germain unmistakably bears the stamp of the Curzonian school of thought'.[20] What emerged as a great zone of buffer states stretching from Scandinavia to India was seen by Strausz-Hupé as 'a European zone of separation between the Eurasian Heartland and the marginal crescent of sea-power'. To Curzon it was more particularly intended to separate the area where British sea power was predominant from that of the predominance of Russian land power.

The dichotomy of land power and sea power was given a new ideological dimension by the Russian Revolution of 1917 and the coming to power of the Bolsheviks. From then on a major pre-occupation of the ruling classes in the capitalist countries was preventing the spread of communism, and Curzon's foreign policy reflects this. For a time Britain and the other major Western powers aligned themselves with the Whites, the opponents of the Bolsheviks, and Western forces were deployed in their support. Russia was thus given treatment of a sort very similar to that meted out at the same time to the three other crumbling Eurasian empires — the Ottomans, Persia and China — and Curzon was at first largely impervious to advice that this was unwise. The partial dismemberment of the old Russian Empire came to be actively pursued and Mackinder's mission of 1919 was a part of this strategy. Curzon always viewed the world geopolitical map as being subject to change and he very much approved of the erasure from it of superannuated states. In 1907 he had referred to them as 'a residue' and talked of the 'scramble for new lands or for the heritage of decaying states'. The weakening of Russia for political, ideological and indeed geopolitical reasons was thus a course of action very much approved of by the Foreign Secretary. In the event it was a policy which proved unsuccessful and had to be rapidly abandoned as an embarrassment. In 1921 Britain became the first great power to recognise the new state, and Curzon was reluctantly obliged to receive the Soviet ambassador to the Court of St James.

Nevertheless, as has been observed, the new state lost a good deal of the European territory of the old Russian Empire, and both Poland and Finland now became independent. The 'Curzon Line', demarcated on linguistic grounds by the British Foreign Office, was proposed as a suitable frontier between Poland and Russia. It accorded with the Wilsonian principles of national self-determination propounded at Versailles and also helped strengthen the East European buffer zone, but in the event the Poles refused to accept it and invaded Russia. As a result the eventual frontier was considerably to the east and was fraught with the sort of problems which Curzon might well have envisaged.

Leo Amery was also at this time an active political figure. A protégé of Milner and a member of the famous 'Kindergarten', he was a Member of Parliament from 1911 to 1945 and was at the Colonial Office for a time when Curzon was Foreign Secretary. Subsequently he became Secretary of State for Dominion Affairs. Like Curzon, he was an active member of the Royal Geographical Society and before World War I had been one of the 'Coefficients' (see Chapter 3). His son, Julian, claimed that he was 'the theoretician of British Imperialism' with a mission to transform the 'rather ramshackle Victorian Empire into an effective Imperial union'.[21] Amery was well acquainted with Mackinder's ideas and his diaries reveal that the two were in broad agreement. Amery was to remain a staunch imperialist throughout his subsequent political career.

Fairgrieve, who had developed a global geopolitical view more comprehensive than any other at the time except for that of Mackinder, was not himself active in politics. Throughout the war and the turbulent post-war years he remained a lecturer at London University's Institute of Education where his influence on the teaching of geography was immense. However, at the time his geopolitical ideas do not appear to have been influential in political circles. H.J. Fleure, writing in 1953 was of the opinion that *Geography and World Power* was 'too forward looking to be properly appreciated in pre-war Britain'.[22] Fleure felt that 'both books' — those of Fairgrieve and Mackinder — 'could have helped Cabinet Ministers to avoid mistakes from which our country is unlikely to recover'. This is reminiscent of Spencer Wilkinson's 'unoccupied space' jibe half a century earlier with its implied reproach to those political leaders who fail to understand the geographical basis upon which successful political action has to be based (see page 29). Fairgrieve's real delight had been in 'sowing seeds' and these seeds, like those of Mackinder, were shortly to land in far more fertile soil across the North Sea in Germany.

Notes

1. L.S. Amery, 'Discussion following the presentation of "The Geographical Pivot of History" by H.J. Mackinder', *Geographical Journal*, 23 (1904).
2. Lord Curzon of Kedleston, *Frontiers* (Clarendon, Oxford, 1908).
3. J. Partsch, *Central Europe* (Frowde, London, 1906).
4. E. Lavisse, *General View of the Political History of Europe* (Longmans Green, London, 1891).
5. P. Vidal de la Blache, *Principles of Human Geography* (Constable, London, 1926).
6. J.A. Froude, *Oceana, or England and her Colonies* (Longman Green, London, 1886).
7. P. Vidal de la Blache, *Principles of Human Geography*, Chapter IV.
8. J. Fairgrieve, *Geography and World Power*, 1st edn (University of London Press, London, 1915).
9. Ibid., Chapter XII.
10. Ibid., Chapter XVII.
11. J. Fairgrieve, *Geography and World Power*, 2nd edn (University of London Press, London, 1919), Chapter XVIII.
12. Ibid., Chapter XIX.
13. V. Cornish, *A Geography of Imperial Defence* (Sifton Praed, London, 1923).
14. E.C. Semple, *Influences of Geographic Environment* (Constable, London, 1914), Chapter VI.
15. J. Fairgrieve, *Geography and World Power*, 1st edn, Chapter X.
16. E.C. Semple, *Influences of Geographic Environment*.
17. Ibid., Chapter XVII.
18. E. Huntington, *Civilization and Climate* (Yale University Press, New Haven, Conn., 1915).
19. Lord Curzon, *Frontiers*.
20. R. Strausz-Hupé, *Geopolitics: The Struggle for Space and Power* (Putnam, New York, 1942).
21. J. Barnes and D. Nicholson (eds.), *The Leo Amery Diaries*, Vol. 1: 1896-1929, introduction by Julian Amery (Hutchinson, London, 1980).
22. H.J. Fleure, 'Obituary of James Fairgrieve', *Geography*, XXXVIII, 4 (1953).

GERMAN *GEOPOLITIK* AND ITS ANTECEDENTS

In the wake of the defeat of November 1918 a wave of black despair gripped the German nation. There was widespread disillusion and cynicism about the policies and the leadership which had precipitated this descent into the abyss. The old certainties had been swept away and replaced by an atmosphere of brooding apprehension. As Kästner had put it: 'We are sitting in a waiting room called Europe. We arc living provisionally.'[1] Such was the magnitude of what had happened that the new condition could not possibly be perceived as being a permanent one. In order to rationalise the disaster there arose myths such as that of the 'stab in the back' of the army by the politicians of the new republic and that of Langemarck in which the German soliders threw themselves at the enemy with magnificent but hopeless heroism.

The bitterness and the shame were all the more intense because in 1914 the German Empire, born barely half a century earlier, had marched out with such confidence to its first major European war. Its rise had been meteoric and by the beginning of the twentieth century it was, both economically and militarily, the most powerful state on the Continent. Now this magnificent edifice had suddenly been replaced by a defeated republic of dubious legitimacy, deprived of armed forces, partially occupied by the enemy,[2] territorially truncated and politically highly divided (Figure 5.1).

It was in this atmosphere of exceptional bleakness in the years following the defeat that *Geopolitik* developed. However, its roots went back to that intellectual tradition which was the legacy of Prussia and the Second Empire. Western-style liberalism had been steadily abandoned in the late nineteenth century and replaced by a growing belief in the ultimate sanction of physical power. 'The triumph of the strong over the weak is the inexorable law of life', Treitschke had proclaimed and, despite all Bismarck's diplomacy, the Second Empire had in fact owed its existence to the physical power of Prussia. With such origins the habit of physical aggrandisement by force of arms came to be ingrained in the new state. The symbiosis of heroic German myths with modern industrial and military power gave birth to a state in which

Figure 5.1: Germany's Frontiers after World War I

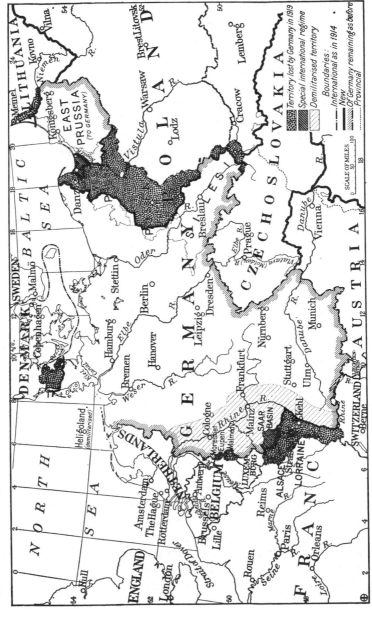

Source: Bowman, J., *The New World* (Harrap & Co. Ltd, London, 1926).

heroism, aggression, power and dominion were deemed to be necessary and justified. As Sombast put it: 'To be a German means to be a hero. Heroism is the natural form of German-Nordic man.'[3] It all contributed to that *gothischer Wahn,* powerfully influenced by Wagner with his return to the ancient Germanic myths of gods and heroes, and by Nietzsche with his obsession with power and his vision of the superman. The self-proclaimed embodiment of this German spirit had been the Kaiser Wilhelm II, a weak and bombastic man with dreams of glory.

Both of these characteristics, the weakness and the search for glory, were reflected in the character of the German national territory and the dangers and possibilities inherent in it. Prussia, as Bismarck had said, was an armed camp in the middle of the plains and its only effective frontiers were its armies. The German Empire after 1871 had inherited both this Prussian sense of vulnerability and its response of aggressive militarism. That *Macht* was the only effective answer to the problems inherent in this *conditio Germaniae* was a view which entered into German geopolitical thinking at an early stage. The favoured territorial concept soon came to be that of a large and powerful *Mitteleuropa,* led by the German Empire. Other German and non-German peoples living in and around the centre of Europe were also to find protection beneath the extended wings of the new Prussian eagle. This would produce a power adequate to deter any predatory ambitions by the other great powers which were seen to be encircling Germany with such menace. Viewed in an even wider spectrum, it could be the only way of preventing that most terrible of all potential disasters, the squeezing out of the German people between the spheres of Russia and Britain, respectively the Behemoth and the Leviathan of the early twentieth century world. Partsch had advocated that all the peoples of Central Europe should unite for their own survival.[4] His *Mitteleuropa* stretched from the Rhine in the west to the Danube in the east, and the control over its peripheries by outside powers had to be brought to an end. Foremost among these outside powers were France and Russia, and Partsch was clearly aware of the historic danger to Germany of war on two fronts: 'The possibility of being simultaneously attacked on both sides lays on the German Empire the burden of heavy military preparation. But as the warlike dispositions of its western and eastern neighbours grow and become more menacing, so do all its members become the more closely knit together.' These other 'members' consisted of those Germans and others, mostly Slavs, whom Partsch considered the German Empire had the right and the duty to organise.

Ten years later the embattled Friedrich Naumann also saw in the war the opportunity for the establishment at last of a strong and united *Mitteleuropa* which would crystallise around its 'mid-European nucleus': 'We must construct our house of the state not with the cedars of Lebanon, but with the building stones of the Roman Capitol.'[5] A few years later Spengler was to echo these sentiments when he observed that Germany might never produce another Goethe but it was essential that she should produce another Caesar.[6] Implicit in this idea of a powerful German Empire within a strong and united *Mitteleuropa* was the eventual unification of all German-speaking peoples. Thus Bismarck's prudent *Kleindeutschland* policy was to be but a stepping stone on the way to a future *Grossdeutschland* which would control the centre of Europe and so be able to rival the truly great powers of the world.

As Germany lay prostrate in the years following the defeat, the rightness of such ideas appeared to many Germans to be increasingly confirmed by the policies of the victors towards their country. Large tracts of the country's eastern territory were detached by the Treaty of Versailles and handed over to Poland, now resurrected as a sovereign state after over a hundred years. East Prussia, in the most heroic and sacred part of the German territory, the place of real and legendary battles against the peoples of the east, was detached from the body of the new German state in order to provide the Poles with their 'corridor' to the sea. At the same time the ancient Hanse town of Danzig became a free city. From the Baltic to the Black Sea the peacemakers had established a *cordon sanitaire* of small states, most of them carved from the corpse of the Austro-Hungarian Empire. As a result of all this, the German people were in a weaker position in Europe after Versailles than they had been for many centuries.

The profound divisions within the new Germany soon resulted in a political vacuum which was to be filled by extremist political parties, in particular the Nazis. They offered a way of overcoming the 'gnawing uncertainty and brooding apprehension' by harking back to a stable but heroic past.[7] They rose to power on the basis of their claim to be both the bringers of social revolution and the restorers of the nation's pride. The new Nietzchean superman,

Adolf Hitler, was to lead the German people out of their black night and into that place in the sun for which that earlier super-man, the Kaiser, had so yearned. However, this time the process of aggrandisement was not to be the hesitant and *ad hoc* one of the past; it was to be rationalised and pursued in a quasi-scientific manner and an important weapon in doing this was *Geopolitik*.

The term *Geopolitik* had been invented by the Swedish political scientist, Rudolf Kjellén (1846-1922). He fully subscribed to the Social Darwinism which had been introduced into political geography by Ratzel. Kjellén's most important work on the subject was *Staten som Lifsform*.[8] He became increasingly interested in the anatomy of power and in its geographical foundations and he defined *Geopolitik* as 'the science which conceives of the state as a geographical organism or as a phenomenon in space'.[9] This state organism was engaged in a perpetual struggle for life and space and it was only the fittest which could survive and prosper. He regarded states as being sensual and rational beings like men, obeying laws of birth, growth, development and decline. Space was seen as being the main key to success and so 'vital vigorous states with limited space obey the categorical political importance of expanding their space by colonisation, amalgamation and con-quest'.

Kjellén's conclusions made him alarmed at what he judged to be the increasingly unfavourable world position of *Mitteleuropa* and in particular of the dangers to his native Sweden arising from Russia's expansionist tendencies. He regarded Sweden on its own, and even his favoured idea of a Scandinavian bloc, as being quite inadequate to save the situation. As a Germanophile, his solution was the invocation of the German Empire as the centre of a future German-Nordic grouping which would have the strength to hold the centre of Europe firm.

To Kjellén, the principal attributes of great power were spaciousness, internal cohesion and ease of external communi-cation. He found Germany to be lacking in each of these, and stressed the need for their acquisition if she were to survive as a power. In his view, this should take the form of an extended central European empire the corner-stones of which were to be Dunkerque, Riga, Hamburg and Baghdad. Such an edifice would have encompassed both the Austro-Hungarian and the Ottoman Empires, and so included also much of the Middle East. He envisaged it as being a kind of *Staatenbund* under German leadership and with a Berlin-Baghdad railroad as its principal internal axis.

Kjellén was, of course, well aware that the British could not possibly have tolerated the emergence of such an empire based on Central Europe with Scandinavia allied to it, and he therefore accepted that eventual conflict with the British Empire was inevitable. He wrote in 1914 that 'England stands today as the last and greatest embodiment of the ancient idea that the oceans of the world must have one master and not several',[10] and called upon Germany to oppose this idea and so to create a new centre of power of global rank.

Calleo maintains that such geopolitical perspectives were the staple substance of German middle class opinion in the years before World War I and that the Germans were not only aggressive against the status quo, but had 'ultimate hegemonic aims'.[11] However, there is little evidence that the ideas of *Geopolitik* were really influential in Germany's international strategy at the time. Overtly expansionist ideas remained peripheral and when aggrandisement did come it appears in the first instance to have been motivated more by expediency than by grand design. There was no Machiavellian plan on the part of the Wilhelmstrasse for the subjugation of Europe and it appears rather to have been a case of *l'appetit vient en mangeant*. The German *Geopolitik* which developed in the 1920s had a far more rational approach to the achievement of national fulfilment. From the beginning it was in the business of both explanation and prescription. There was the explanation of how the disaster had ever been allowed to take place at all, and the prescription for how Germany could once again be restored to her rightful place in Europe. The study of spatial reality was to be used to shed light on the German predicament and spatial remedies were to be administered to the sickly, but soon remarkably co-operative, patient.

It was in Munich that *Geopolitik* originated and developed in the years after World War I, and it was always especially associated with this city although it later came to be studied at many German universities. Weigert commented on the particularly intense atmosphere in those years and pointed out that 'Munich had always been the intellectual cauldron in which fantastic and mysterious German concoctions were brewed'.[12] Spengler, Hitler and Haushofer all lived and worked in this city which was also the home of German National Socialism.

The central figure in German *Geopolitik* was Professor Karl Haushofer (1869–1946), the son of a Bavarian schoolmaster who rose to the rank of Major-General in the Imperial army. He travelled widely and cultivated a lifelong interest in the Far East and especially in Japan. This latter country was to recur over the years as one of his most favoured geopolitical models. Like Kjellén before him, he became increasingly absorbed in the relationship between geography and political activity and was convinced that the location and territorial characteristics of states were the principal determinants of their destiny. He was instrumental in establishing the *Institut für Geopolitik* in Munich, and in 1924 became the first editor of its journal, *Zeitschrift für Geopolitik*. Subsequently *Facts in Review,* published in English, was to inform students in the Anglo-Saxon countries of the kind of geopolitical ideas which were emanating from Munich. This was, of course, largely propaganda which attempted to put *Geopolitik* in the best possible light for overseas consumption. The Munich institute soon became the recognised centre for the study of the subject and Karl Haushofer remained its principal exponent. His son Albrecht, a friend of Rudolf Hess, also became a geopolitician, and appears to have helped introduce *Geopolitik* to the Nazi hierarchy. Other significant geopoliticians working in Munich and at other centres included Ewald Banse, Wulf Siewert, Colin Ross, Johannes Kühn, Richard Hennig and Kurt Vowinckel.

The *Geopolitik* developed at Munich was a sort of synthesis of history, economics, politics and the physical sciences all welded together through the application of a spatial and territorial perspective. It was *Wissenschaft und Kunst*[13] and its object was to achieve an understanding of the dynamic working of the state through the observation of its morphology and the interactions of its components. While the principal objective from the beginning was a fuller understanding of the nature of that *conditio Germaniae,* it was concerned with the whole world and particular sections were set up for the study of the United States, Latin America and the Far East. After the coming to power of the Nazis in 1933 the *Institut für Geopolitik* was accorded official recognition at the highest levels. After this it became less objective and that cloak of academic respectability, which had been regarded as its major asset, was gradually discarded in favour of a closer identification with the policies of the Third Reich.

The ideas upon which German *Geopolitik* was based had been

strongly influenced by those of political geographers outside the German-Nordic world and in particular by those of the Anglo-Saxon countries. A favourite saying of Haushofer, who was partial to Latin quotations, was Ovid's *fas est ab hoste doceri*.[14] He had a particular reverence for Mackinder, upon whose ideas many of his own were based (Figure 5.2). Mackinder's 1904 article, to which he often referred, he considered to be 'the greatest of all geographical world views': 'Never have I seen anything greater than these few pages of geopolitical masterwork.'[15] As has been noted, Mahan had been a well known and much respected figure in Imperial Germany and his ideas on sea power had been carefully studied. Fairgrieve's *Geography and World Power* was translated into German by Haushofer's wife Martha and was published with an introduction by Haushofer in 1925.[16]

Karl Haushofer was himself a most prolific writer, producing a stream of books and articles and, of course, editing the *Zeitschrift*. The subjects he covered range widely, but he always retained his particular interest in the Far East. Works of particular importance include *Das Japanische Reich in seiner geographischen Entwickelung*,[17] *Die Geopolitik des Pazifischen Ozeans*,[18] *Geopolitik der Panideen*[19] and *Weltpolitik von Heute*.[20] He was to remain until the end the presiding genius and father figure of *Geopolitik* although in the course of time other strands developed which had different emphases and even alternative viewpoints. Nevertheless, it is quite possible to view *Geopolitik* as a whole and to detect the recurrence of methods and themes throughout the period between the wars.

Its protagonists claimed that it was a scientific method for arranging geographical data so as to develop a spatial *Weltanschauung* and that it used the methods of both reason and intuition — *Wissenschaft und Kunst* — in arriving at its conclusions. In the manner of Social Darwinism, the state was seen as an organism having the characteristics outlined by Kjellén. In the perpetuation of its existence the state has many needs, none more fundamental than that of *Lebensraum*, living space, and its growth and development is dependent upon the availability of this. This *Grossraum* will in turn give it greater dynamism with which to effect an anthropogeographical domination of its space, and the dissemination of the national *Kultur* is the most effective method of space conquest. The state must always justify the acquisition of yet more *Lebensraum* by demonstrating its ability to use that which it already possesses. In doing this the dynamic state will also achieve

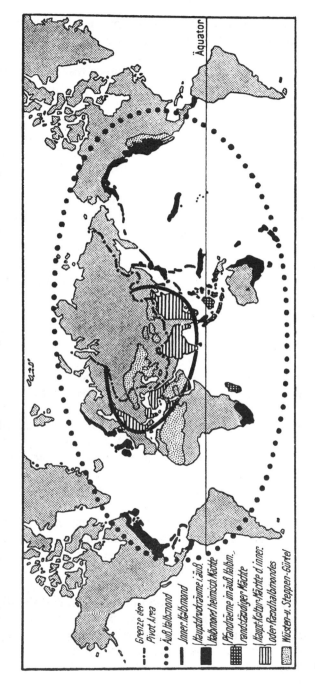

Figure 5.2: Mackinder's Pivot Map as adapted by Haushofer. This demonstrates the confrontation of land and sea power in the world. The Inner Hemisphere (*Inner. Halbmond*) with its higher civilisation (including the German) is opposed by the major centres of maritime pressure (*Hauptdruckräume*) around its fringes.

Äquator

Grenze den Pivot Area
Äuß.Halbmond
Inner.Halbmond
Hauptdruckräume i.äuß.
Halbmond heimisch.Mächte
Pandsteme im äuß.Halbm.-
randständiger Mächte
Haupt-Kultan-Nächte d.inner.
Loden-Randhalbmondes
Wüsten-u. Steppen-Gürtel

Source: Haushofer, K., *Jenseits Der Grossmächte* (B.G. Teubner, Leipzig, 1932).

greater economic autarchy and become increasingly independent of its neighbours. The possession of such freedom is the hallmark of the truly great power. The national space has also to be protected by secure frontiers and the larger the territory the more effective this defence is likely to be. The key features of the spatial structure of the state, which he called the 'geopolitical manometers', also have a role in the successful growth of the state. They include the capital, the centre of gravity of the state, the power fields, cultural dynamics and marginal growth. A great power also needs an internal axis which will be the major line of development of its strength. Dynamic states will inevitably absorb smaller ones lying in their way which have not been able to develop successful political structures. These are the *Kleinstaatengerümpel* which have often in the past hampered the growth of great powers. The remaining states, far fewer in number, will eventually be forced into conflict with one another over the possession of territory.

In addition to this primary urge for *Lebensraum* there is also a basic drive towards the sea — *navigare necesse est.*[21] This was because the sea was seen as the source of wealth derived from commerce and thus of additional strength to the state. It was also contended that far from being a divider, as was commonly believed, the sea was in fact a force for unity, and so its possession was a stepping stone to further expansion. Haushofer, quoting Ratzel, said: 'Only the sea can bring out real world powers. The step across the sea is the most notable event in any nation's history.'[22] This was clearly a view shared by Siewert, who wrote that 'the influence of land power ends as a rule at its boundaries, but the influence of sea power may extend across the whole earth'.[23] Nevertheless, it was acknowledged that land power had to take precedence over sea power and needed to be consolidated before sea power could be sought after.

The dynamic state needed not just to expand, but to expand intelligently into the optimum territory best able to cater for its requirements. It was essential that geography be made into an ally and not an enemy. Here Haushofer contrasted the success of the Roman Empire, which had made geography its ally, with the failure of Napoleon, who had not. Successful expansion in the modern world will eventually lead to the formation of large states making geographical sense. Haushofer referred to these as 'Pan-regions' and they needed to be territorially large, self-sufficient in raw materials and to possess the right geopolitical manometers.[24]

They should for preference be longitudinal rather than latitudinal so as to have a large range of natural regions within their extended boundaries (Figure 5.3).

As has been observed, Haushofer's *Weltanschauung* was derived from that of Mackinder, and the *Geopolitiker* fully accepted the thesis of the world conflict of land and sea power. This, said Haushofer, 'was a powerful age-old *Leitmotiv*... which sets the pattern of present-day world politics just as it did in the days of the Greeks and the Romans'.[25] It had been 'one of the most pervasive phenomena of geopolitics' and it had not only set nation against nation, but had even divided countries. Haushofer gave France as an example of a country under considerable strain because of the opposing demands of the continental and the maritime.

Land and sea power operated in totally different ways and so could not readily be compared. März saw this demonstrated in the way in which each approached the acquisition of space:

> Seapower masters great spaces by leaping lightly from point to point. Seapower husbands its strength and seeks to gain with the least effort the greatest advantages by the subtle adaptation to existing conditions. Seapower inclines, therefore, to compromise and even to concede, whenever possible, a degree of self-rule to its possessions. It delays pressing its formal claims to a territory or marine area as long as these can be controlled through dependent or allied states. Landpower by contrast advances methodically, seeks to establish its control by thorough organisation and, above all, to preserve the mobility of its forces.[26]

It followed from this that a land power was most effective on land and a sea power when at sea and both far less so when venturing into the element of the other. Since this inhibited them both from a complete mastery, Haushofer concluded that the ideal would be a power which was equally at home on land and sea, able to use its mastery of the land to turn successfully to control of the sea.

Geopolitik was thus founded on environmental determinism since it was sustained by the belief that the power to which any state can attain is dependent upon its geographical circumstances. The people of a dynamic state are in a sense 'chosen' for their conquering mission, but more by the character of their physical

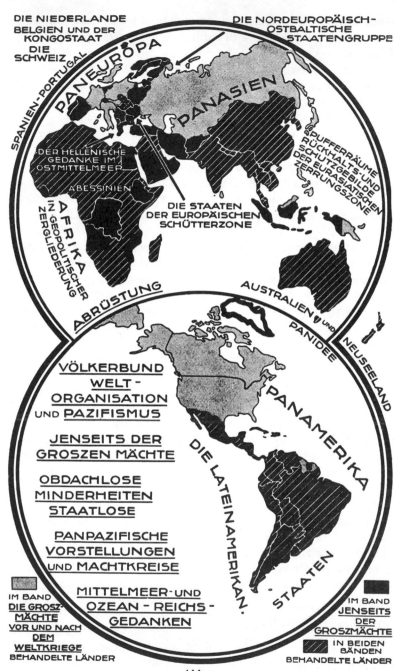

DIE NIEDERLANDE
BELGIEN UND DER
KONGOSTAAT
DIE
SCHWEIZ

SPANIEN-PORTUGAL

PANEUROPA

DIE NORDEUROPÄISCH-
OSTBALTISCHE
STAATENGRUPPE

PANASIEN

PUFFERRÄUME
RÜCKHALTS-UND
SCHUTZGEBILDE
DER EURASIATISCHEN
ZERRUNGSZONE

DER HELLENISCHE
GEDANKE IM
OSTMITTELMEER

ABESSINIEN

AFRIKA IN GEOPOLITISCHER ZERGLIEDERUNG

DIE STAATEN
DER EUROPÄISCHEN
SCHÜTTERZONE

ABRÜSTUNG

AUSTRALIEN UND

PANIDEE

NEUSEELAND

VÖLKERBUND
WELT-
ORGANISATION
UND **PAZIFISMUS**

**JENSEITS DER
GROSZEN MÄCHTE**

**OBDACHLOSE
MINDERHEITEN
STAATLOSE**

**PANPAZIFISCHE
VORSTELLUNGEN**
UND **MACHTKREISE**

MITTELMEER-UND
**OZEAN - REICHS -
GEDANKEN**

PANAMERIKA

DIE LATEINAMERIKAN.

STAATEN

IM BAND
**DIE GROSZ-
MÄCHTE**
VOR UND NACH
DEM
WELTKRIEGE
BEHANDELTE LÄNDER

IM BAND
**JENSEITS
DER
GROSZMÄCHTE**

IN BEIDEN
BÄNDEN
BEHANDELTE LÄNDER

Abb. 1.

environment than by the particular race to which they happen to belong. Despite this, it was inevitable that with the coming to power of the Nazis, racialism would creep in. Haushofer himself contributed to this by making the distinction between the *Raumüberwindende* and the *Raumgebundende* races. The white, and in particular the Teutonic, races naturally dominated the former category. Yet he showed himself to be well aware of the contradiction between his environmentalism and Nazi-style racialism, and this was nowhere more evident than in his considerable admiration for Japan. On a number of occasions he warned of the danger of mistaken racial prejudices.

Although it was space rather than race which was the principal determinant of national destiny, it was considered that the inhabitants of a favoured location would develop particular qualities as they responded to the call to greatness: 'The expansive vigour of the human will invariably asserts itself in a process of political space domination.'[27] The whole process was to be set in motion by the emergence of great leaders, Nietzschean supermen, able to discern geopolitical reality and to be the instruments for the fulfilment of geopolitical destiny. This was the *Führerprinzip* which was so fundamental to Nazi dogma.

Geopolitik was, then, equipped with a theoretical structure for explaining the spatial dynamics of power. The task which Haushofer always saw before him was that of shedding light on the realities which lay behind Germany's world situation. To this task he and his colleagues brought a strong emotional commitment and considerable urgency. The position of Germany after the Treaty of Versailles was to him nothing short of appalling: 'The mutilation of our national soil is unbearable', he wrote, and the new frontiers were 'the festering wounds of a national body's outer skin' produced when parts had been torn from the national territory.[28] These lands had to be returned to Germany and in the longer term the whole German *Volk* had to be united into a single state. German scholars had rarely found the concepts of 'German' and 'Germany' easy ones to come to terms with. In the indeterminate

Figure 5.3: Pan Ideas according to Haushofer, 1931, showing the great powers of the present (*Groszmächte*) and of the future (*Jenseits*) together with the Pan Ideas (*Panideen*).

Source: As in Figure 5.2.

geographical conditions of Central Europe, the nation did not slot into its physical environment with the kind of ease found in countries like France. Concepts such as *Volksboden, Sprachboden* and *Kulturboden* could be very difficult to express cartographically (Figure 5.4).[29] They all had a further relationship with the even more amorphous concept of *Mitteleuropa* which was by no means entirely German but had come to be regarded as being in some way predestined for German domination. Heber saw the German people as being 'entrusted with the eternal task of keeping order in the Central European space ... This task of the Reich will exist as long as there is a German people that derives its historic mission out of the nature of its space'.[30]

From this strong Central European base, the natural direction of German expansion in search of *Lebensraum* was towards the east. This implied a new *Drang nach Osten* and that maritime

Figure 5.4: The German *Volksboden* and *Kulturboden* in *Mitteleuropa*

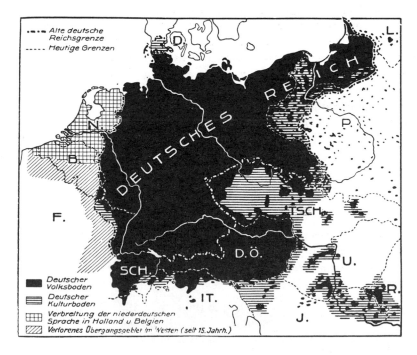

Source: Haushofer, K., *Raumüberwindende Mächte* (B.G. Teubner, Leipzig, 1934).

imperialism on the western model, after which the Kaiser had hankered when he asserted that Germany's future lay on the water, had to be renounced in favour of the continental policy for which Germany was far better equipped. While Imperial Germany, according to Haushofer, had been the strongest power on the continent it had been at the same time the weakest of the world powers. This had also been the opinion of Kjellén who attributed this weakness to Germany's inability to secure control over her external communications. To the *Geopolitiker* the huge territories stretching to the east were Germany's *Schicksalsraum*. The Treaty of Versailles had erected a barrier consisting of small and artificial states, *Kleinstaatengerümpel*, to curtail Germany's natural expansion in that direction (Figure 5.5). What to the French and the British was a *cordon sanitaire*, designed to keep Germany and Russia apart, was to the *Geopolitiker* a hated *Teufelsgürtel* around their country. It had to be the object of Germany's eastern policy to destroy this and ensure that it was replaced by a German-dominated system. The stress in the writings of the 1930s was on co-operation with the non-German peoples of the region who were considered to be 'European' in a way that the Russians most decidedly were not. The German role should be that of developing with them a new and higher form of politico-economic organisation. 'Should not the natural and mutually advantageous relationship of the eastern peoples to Germany be that of symbiosis?' enquired Kühn, rather ominously, in 1940.[31]

This European strategy advocated by the *Geopolitiker* was to be pursued in the context of the world domination of the great maritime and continental powers — 'the pirates of the steppe and the pirates of the sea'. Both were the natural enemies of German aspirations and together they were considered to have been responsible for having converted the centre of the continent into Europe's *Zerrungszone*. Together they had barred Germany's attempts to gain outlets to the west and to gain territory in the east. The two were engaged, in accordance with Mackinder's thesis, in their own *Raumstreben* particularly in the Eastern Mediterranean, the Middle East and Southern Asia. It was this underlying conflict which gave some cause for hope, as it had been the temporary alliances of land and sea power which, as during World War I, had produced the times of greatest danger for Germany.

Of the two, it was the British Empire which during the 1920s was identified by the *Geopolitiker* as the principal enemy and the

Figure 5.5: European Power Groupings and the Danger to
Germany, 1931, showing Germany, significantly grouped with
Austria as *Deutsche Staaten*, surrounded by the French sphere of
influence (*Französische Einflussphäre*). To the south is the Italian
sphere and to the east that of the Soviet Union which,
interestingly, includes Lithuania.

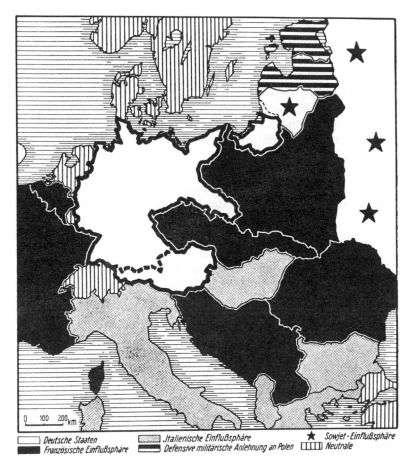

| Deutsche Staaten | Italienische Einflußsphäre | ★ Sowjet-Einflußsphäre |
| Französische Einflußsphäre | Defensive militärische Anlehnung an Polen | Neutrale |

Source: As in Figure 5.2.

one which would need to be confronted first. Looked at geopolitically, World War I was seen to have been a massive victory
for maritime power, led by the British Empire, and an equally
shattering defeat for the principal continental powers. The British

Empire represented universalism and had secured its world power through economic and political liberalism. While its system presented a façade of benign tolerance towards the rest of the world, Haushofer saw this as a ruse for securing maximum British advantage and drew attention rather to the 'anaconda policy'. A 'suggestive map' published in the *Zeitschrift* shows the tentacles of the British Empire extending into all parts of the world, even the Soviet Union (Figure 5.6). As the 1920s wore on, the coupling of the Americans with British interests through the use of the term 'Anglo-Saxon' implied an acknowledgement of the weakening of Britain's world grip and the growing importance of the United States. The League of Nations, led by Britain and the 'lesser maritime powers' was seen as being another device for the preservation of the British Empire by freezing the global order into its early twentieth century pattern. 'After they [the Western powers] had held up the world, they asked the world to stop further holdups.'[32]

The new world order which had been blessed and legitimised at Versailles was thus totally rejected by the *Geopolitiker* and exposed as being Western hypocrisy. The response which was proposed was that of the search for an *entente* with the Soviet Union. This 'softly, softly' approach to the *Drang nach Osten* followed from the conviction that Germany's true destiny lay in the east, but the tactics were conditioned by the international situation in the 1920s. The Soviet Union was now seen as being another pariah nation which had also been geographically mutilated and then rejected by the West. Together, said Haushofer, the two powers could form the 'continental union of the expelled against the sea-ruling world-power in the League of Nations'.[33]

There was also a third strand to the proposed eastern policy and this was in the Far East. As has been seen, Japan had always been one of Haushofer's principal loves and fascinations. He now watched the rise of Japanese imperial power with much admiration and he saw in Japan a state from which Germany could learn a great deal. At an early stage he became convinced that Japan had to be a friend and not an enemy in his country's challenge to the hateful Anglo-American hegemony. Earlier he had written that together Japan, Russia and the Central European Imperial Power would be absolutely unassailable' as they were 'the only group of powers able to defend itself against the Anglo-Saxon tutelage'.[34] Thus Haushofer was very much a man of Rapallo[35] and in 1939 he was to be equally enthusiastic over the Nazi-Soviet pact.[36] To him

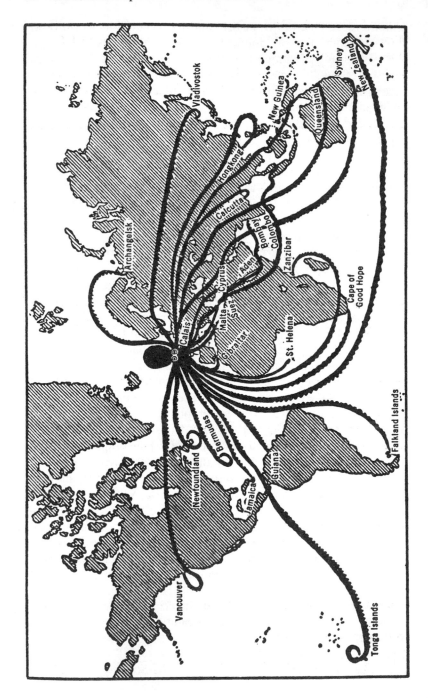

Figure 5.7 (below): The Extent of *Mitteleuropa. Mitteleuropa* (Der *Mitteleuropäische Raum*) here extends over those areas left unshaded. Territory in *Mitteleuropa* occupied by peoples living under alien rule is shaded in black. The largest proportion of these are Germans but there are also numbers of Ukrainians and Hungarians.

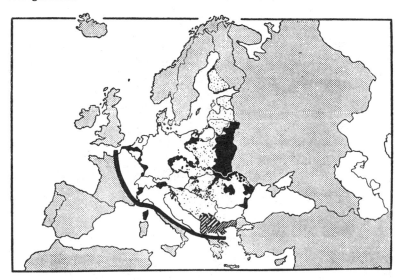

Source: As in Figure 5.2.

these alliances gave Germany security and the possibility of dominance in her *Schicksalsraum* and they were steps on the road towards that great continental system towards which he was aiming. He held to the conviction that it was conflict between Germany and Russia which had enabled the Western powers to secure their world hegemony and that this must be a lesson to them both for the future. In 1939 Haushofer attempted to reconcile this with the *Drang nach Osten* by advising rather obscurely that 'they should not again endanger, by ideological differences,

Figure 5.6 (left): A Suggestive Map of the British Empire, which gives the general impression that Vladivostok and Archangelsk also form part of the British Empire.

Source: Dorpalen, A., *The World of General Haushofer* (Farrar & Rinehart, Inc., New York, 1942).

the geopolitical foundations of their adjustable space existence'.[37]

This concern with Russia was further heightened by the importance of the Heartland in their geopolitical thinking. Russia, now transformed into the Soviet Union, was regarded as being no more than its '*de facto* tenant'. Haushofer knew Mackinder's famous triptych well, and had digested the pronouncements of the airy cherub concerning the key role of Eastern Europe and consequently of the power which could secure control over it. Yet he foresaw great danger in attempting to secure the Heartland by force of arms. To him the lesson of Napoleon was a most salutary one: geography must be an ally and not an enemy. It followed from this that the domination of the Heartland should be achieved by diplomacy and stealth rather than by attempted conquest. Others among the *Geopolitiker* were less cautious than this and envisaged the necessity of war in the east as part of the process of Germany's rise to world power. Yet despite these considerable differences in the tactics, all were basically united on the goal. As Strausz-Hupé put it, the question was whether to 'lure the bear with honey or to stalk him gun in hand'.[38] In other words, was it to be Rapallo or Brest-Litovsk?[39]

Here we come to the question of the precise delimitation of the *Lebensraum*. There was frequent temporising on this point, depending on the state of international relations at any particular time. However, it could not be concealed that it lay well to the east of *Mitteleuropa* even when this was stretched to its furthest limits (Figure 5.7). The geopolitical vision was certainly not of the populous lands of Central and Eastern Europe but of the great empty spaces of the Ukraine and the Russian steppes. These possessed the potential for producing food, energy and the raw materials of industry and for taking the surplus population from the small and congested homeland. The Treaty of Brest-Litovsk had detached the Ukraine and other territories from Russia and, although its provisions were only in operation for barely six months, it was considered by many to be a precedent for the future. In *Mein Kampf*[40] Adolf Hitler envisaged future German dominance over huge tracts of land in the East which he considered as being a prerequisite for Germany's status as a great power. It has often been asserted, although it has not been proved, that the philosophy of *Geopolitik*, and even possibly Karl Haushofer himself, influenced the development of Hitler's thinking in this respect. Whether this was so or not, it was the alternative policy of the Eurasian partnership which was the mainstream of both geopolitical thinking emanating from Munich and the policy of the Wilhelmstrasse until well after the commencement of World War II.

It was his powerful alliance of continental states, seen as being like a great citadel 'from the Elbe to the Amur', which would give Germany the strength for her global challenge to the British Empire. Britain had always been seen as the principal power of the Western liberal world system and so the major obstacle to be overcome. However, the examination of the foundations of British power increasingly led them to the conclusion that by the 1930s it was past its historic peak. The Empire's vast size, geographical fragmentation and heterogeneity made it increasingly unwieldy and difficult to control. The Statute of Westminster[41] appeared to confirm the earlier conclusions that the British were looking for ways to shore it up. The roles of the League of Nations and of the United States had been seen in a similar light. Haushofer said of the British Empire: 'Its space mastery is not uncontested ... It has become one of the most problematical political structures of our time.'[42] This led him to predict its disintegration as a consequence

Figure 5.8: The Key Position of India in the British Empire. The dominant position held by Britain throughout the Indian Ocean area is made very clear.

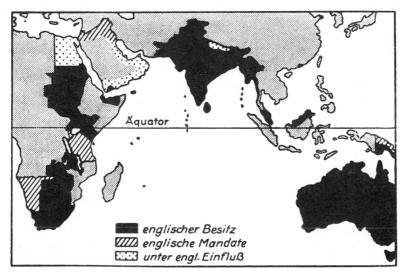

Source: As in Figure 5.2:

of 'geopolitical saturation' — a failure to exert full control over its massive and far-flung territories. A further weakness was the great length of the land frontiers which the British now had to defend. This was most striking in the case of India, and the whole process of continentalisation was demonstrated by the transfer of the capital of the Indian Empire in 1924 from the British-developed port of Calcutta to the Moghul capital deep in the interior at Delhi. To Pahl,[43] India was Britain's key possession and the major imperial leitmotiv was 'the protection of the route from the English motherland to the treasure house of India'. He continued: 'The British Empire lacks cohesion but its centre of gravity is in the Indian Ocean which forms a British inland sea' (Figure 5.8). Haushofer in similar vein had described India evocatively as 'the golden fringe on the Asiatic beggar's cloak'[44] and the principal source of British imperial strength.

Air power was regarded by the *Geopolitiker* as being another development disadvantageous to Britain. They argued that this favoured continental rather than maritime states since it enabled the former to strike at vulnerable points which had formerly been out of range of land-based power. They had in mind principally the Middle East and Southern Asia, but even more ominous was their perception of the new vulnerability of Britain itself to air strikes from the continent. This indicated to them that the era of 'splendid isolation' was now coming to its end. Haushofer expressed the opinion that in effect Britain had ceased to be an island and was in course of being reduced to the level of continental powers like France.

Largely based upon his analysis of the inherent weaknesses of the British Empire, Haushofer concluded that the age of the dominance of sea power as a whole was now coming to an end and that the future lay with land power. He recognised, however, that the maritime powers could not be expected to concede that the geopolitical balance of power was now moving against them, and so conflict would be inevitable before the new age could fully come into being. Despite her growing weakness, he still saw Britain as being the principal 'resisting power' and so the major confrontation would take place with her. Before this took place 'continental questions' would need first to be settled with France.

The fall of the British and the lesser maritime empires was regarded as being a prerequisite for the establishment of the new German-dominated European order. This was itself to be a part of the new world system of regions based upon *Panideen.* 'Without ideological content imperialism soon dies off', said Haushofer, and he defined the *Panideen* as 'supernational all-englobing ideas seeking to manifest themselves in space'.[45] Principal amongst these were the Pan-American, Pan-Asiatic, Pan-Russian, Pan-Pacific, Pan-Islamic and, of course, Pan-European ideas. Their exact territorial extent was at first left rather nebulous since many of them could be expected to establish claim to the same space (Figure 5.3). It was sufficient that the new world order could be expected to come into being through their crystallisation around a number of regional nuclei and they would extend out from these. The one feature which they had in common was their opposition to the universalist claims of the European empires. Eventually, under the pressure of events, the outlines of these *Grosslebensformen* became clearer and some were subsumed into others. By 1941 the three principal ones were Pan-America, led by the United States, Greater East Asia led by Japan, and Pan-Europe led by Germany (Figure 5.9). It is interesting that in the 1941 version, produced before the German invasion of the Soviet Union, and while the Nazi-Soviet Pact was still in operation, Pan-Europe stopped at the Russian frontier. Thus it corresponded quite closely to what Haushofer had referred to as 'the real eastern frontier of Europe' from Lake Peipus to the lower Dniester. It incorporated the Mediterranean, the Middle East and the whole of Africa, and the term 'Eurafrica' had sometimes been used as a natural *Grosslebensform.* These 1941 Pan-regions were thus very large and they incorporated a number of putative lesser Pan-regions of earlier thinking. Since they were aligned longitudinally they contained a number of natural regions and so were thought of as being potentially self-sufficient. Physically they were well separated from one another and consequently easily defensible. The diffusion of American, German and Japanese cultures within each was to act as the human cement for holding such vast areas together. It was also envisaged that, for a time at least, there would be something of a world balance of power among them. The Pan-regions of 1941 had a number of other interesting features, one of which was that the United States was separated from Great Britain. During the 1930s the two countries had increasingly come to be regarded less as natural allies in the creation of an Anglo-Saxon world order than as potential rivals in such an order. In the late 1930s the Americans had therefore been encouraged to join up with

Figure 5.9: The Pan Ideas in 1941.

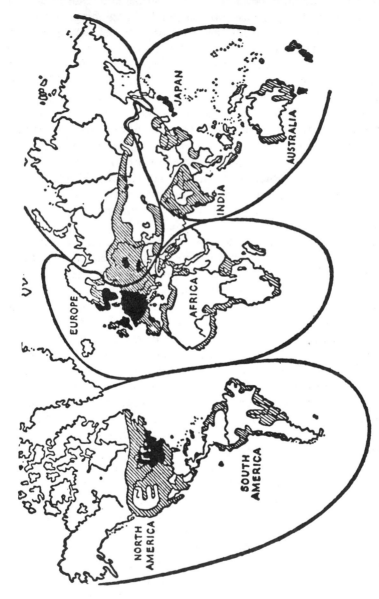

Source: Strausz-Hupé, *World Affairs* (Arno Press, New York, 1972).

Germany and to add their considerable strength to that of the Axis powers.[46] Thus the United States as collaborator with Britain to maintain world hegemony is replaced by the United States as centre of its own Pan-region consisting of the whole of the Western Hemisphere. The United States was encouraged right up to 1941 to dissociate herself from the perpetuation of British-style universalism and to keep out of European affairs. Although America had always held a peripheral place in the grand strategy of *Geopolitik*, there had been widespread admiration for the American giant as having the sort of power towards which Germany aspired. It was regarded as being a geopolitically adjusted power with the right manometers and with a future in the new post-imperial order. Furthermore, the Monroe Doctrine[47] was considered to have been an early example of the sort of anti-universalist regional system which Germany envisaged, as a start at any rate, for Europe.

The Soviet Union, so much the object of territorial acquisition in the *Lebensraum* strategies, was entirely left out of the Pan-regional scheme. This, of course, was during another of those periods when the bear was being lured with honey, an approach which had always been favoured by Haushofer. Its exclusion from any other sphere would imply its constituting a fourth world Pan-region. Earlier versions had given Pan-Russia a longitudinal axis like the others and had extended it through part of the Middle East as far as the Indian Ocean. This was intended to give it a greater range of natural regions and consequent self-sufficiency in natural resources. However, even in the 1941 version, its total area, resources and defensibility allowed it to rank alongside the others. Communism was also seen by some *Geopolitiker* as a sort of pan-idea not dissimilar to the others in its spatial effects and aspirations. Gyorgy was of the opinion that there was no great difference between the philosophies of the Nazis and the communists. The *Geopolitiker* 'had substituted the geographical determinism of Haushofer for the economic materialism of Marx'.[48] The one was concerned with the dialectics of social forces and the other with the dialectics of space and the natural environment. However, such notions of geopolitical coexistence never came easily to the Nazi hierarchy. The 'Jewish-Bolshevik conspiracy' was the great composite world enemy of the Third Reich, and, besides, the Russian ecumene was most uncomfortably close to *Mitteleuropa* itself.

A third feature of the 1941 map was the inclusion of the Mediterranean as a sort of strategic link between Europe, Africa and the Middle East. It had not escaped the notice of the *Geopolitiker* that the Mediterranean was their ally Mussolini's *Mare Nostrum*, his *Schicksalsraum* for the creation of a new Roman Empire centring on Fascist Italy. The aspirations of the Italian dictator were fully appreciated and a number of articles on the subject had appeared in *Zeitschrift* over the years.[49] Nevertheless, the *Drang nach dem Süden* had at least as historic a lineage as did the *Drang nach Osten* and the two, in fact, complemented one another strategically by securing the exposed flanks of *Mitteleuropa*. It was maintained by Haushofer that the failure of numerous conquerors through the ages to establish control over Europe could be attributed to a failure to secure control of the Mediterranean first. In any case, Italian aspirations received little credence in Munich, partly because of a Teutonic contempt for the martial abilities of the Latin peoples and, even more, because they were all too well aware of how fragile was the Italian economic base. The most that realistically appeared to be on offer was that of an Italy controlling the Mediterranean basin as one of the favoured satellite states of *Grossdeutschland*.

Following the German attack on Russia in June 1941, the writers of *Geopolitik* moved back to earlier positions on the fate of the Soviet Union in Germany's New Order. Concern with Eurafrica was again replaced by an emphasis on Eurasia as the 'natural' sphere for German expansion. The German *Kulturboden* was now shown as stretching as far as a line drawn from Leningrad to Odessa, and this implied a dominating Germanic influence over the whole of an area which included the Baltic States, Byelorussia and the Dnieper basin. *Lebensraum* in the east had once more attained the position of the central aim and justification for German expansionism. Russia was to be pushed back into her Muscovite heartland where she would be easy prey for the next stage of German advance into Asia.

Geopolitik was, of course, principally concerned with the role of Germany in the new world order but, as has been observed, Haushofer was himself more interested than were some of the others in developments in the Far East. For him the 'Indo-Pacific space' would be the major centre of power in the future and was destined to replace Europe as the principal arbiter of the world's affairs. He foresaw a gigantic struggle taking place there between four great world powers. These were the British Empire, Russia,

America and Japan, and Haushofer was convinced in his view that it was the latter power which Germany should support. This would give Germany a powerful Asiatic ally having similar geopolitical interests which would help her to achieve her joint world ambitions of bringing about the dismemberment of the British Empire and of securing a dominant position in Eurasia. In seeking to reach these goals, he felt that Germany must ally herself, in the short term, with the new Asiatic nationalisms, in particular that of India, and so replace British influence with her own. Apart from such measures as these, he maintained that Germany should steer clear of the Indo-Pacific space, at least for the time being.

The strategies advocated by the *Geopolitiker* for the achievement of a dominant position for Germany were subject to constant modification right up to World War II. This arose both from the constantly changing international situation and from developing perceptions of global geopolitical realities. The earlier pre-occupation had been with the build-up of German sea power so that it would be in a position to mount a successful challenge to the might of the British Empire. As the British Empire was seen to weaken, then alternative methods came to be advocated for giving it, together with the rest of the maritime world, the *coup de grâce*. It was then that the eastern policy really came into its own. Rather than being merely a source of extra resources, it now came to be seen as an alternative geopolitical system which could free Germany and the rest of the continent from dependence on the sea. With the steady decline in world sea power and the corresponding increase in that of the land aided by the new air power, the whole world geopolitical situation was in course of rapid transformation. By the middle of the 1930s the world tide was seen to be moving strongly in Germany's favour and this needed to be used with some urgency so as to secure that pre-eminence which had seemed almost inconceivable in that bleak time barely 15 years previously.

During the five years between the remilitarisation of the Rhineland in 1936 and the invasion of Russia in the summer of 1941, geopolitical theory had in many ways been translated into practical action. With deceptive ease Germany came into possession of a European empire of staggering proportions and, with the sole important exception of Britain, a German-dominated Pan-Europe had been largely achieved. However, from the winter of 1941-2 onwards the underlying difficulties rapidly surfaced and the true magnitude of the self-proclaimed European mission became apparent. The last three years of the war was a sorry tale of failure to consolidate what had been won and steady erosion of the grossly overextended frontiers. In 1945, for the second time in the century, the German bid for European hegemony ended in catastrophic defeat. With it went the geopolitical concept of *Mitteleuropa*, upon which it was based, and the idea of an autonomous centre of power in the heart of Europe.[50] Karl Haushofer himself, increasingly disillusioned by the Third Reich which had done so much to promote his ideas, committed suicide in 1946.

Is it, then, possible to conclude from this analysis that it was the ideas of *Geopolitik* which were instrumental in causing the *Götterdämmerung* of the Third Reich in May 1945? In the opinion of Strausz-Hupé, it did indeed provide 'the blueprint for world conquest'.[51] He saw *Geopolitik* as 'the master plan that tells what and why to conquer, guiding the military strategist along the easiest path to conquest. Thus the key to Hitler's global mind is geopolitics.' In the broadest sense this may well have been so and, of course, it must be remembered that Strausz-Hupé was writing during World War II. Looking back, it may be observed that many of the policies pursued by the Third Reich with such vigour were actually not those which had been advocated by the *Geopolitiker*. To Haushofer, it was the Western powers which were the main enemies to German hegemonial aspirations. The eastern policy was designed to build up a countervailing force by an alliance of those powers which had been excluded from the Western world system. Underlying it was the Mackinder dichotomy as seen from the viewpoint of the landsman. When the 'anaconda grip' had been loosened then the age of sea power would be replaced by a new world order dominated by land power. Such an eventually had been foreseen all too clearly by Mackinder himself and could only be prevented if the maritime powers took firm and urgent action.

The development of Nazi foreign policy after 1933 took, in fact, a very different perspective from this. The order of priority was the consolidation of a German-dominated *Mitteleuropa* followed by the consolidation of *Lebensraum* in the East. The *Drang nach Osten* drove straight into the Ukraine and, given the methods employed, it was inevitable that it was the Soviet Union which became the principal enemy. It was clearly impossible for two great powers to possess the same *Raum* at the same time. Maritime conquest was thus to be firmly subordinated to continental conquest, and the policy adopted towards Western Europe was, initially at least, largely defensive. The preferred strategy was to seek an arrangement with Britain and France rather than a conflict. In this Britannia was to be allowed to continue to rule the waves so long as Germany was given a free hand in Central and Eastern Europe.

Events, however, were to prove that Britain was not prepared to connive at Germany's dominance of Europe and in particular at the dismemberment of the 'Third Tier' which she had helped to establish after World War I. Britain's behaviour in respect of Germany was thus to be not what the German government hoped, but what Haushofer had long predicted. The Nazi-Soviet Pact of 1939 followed by the European War of 1939–41 brought the international situation for a time closer into line with the principal thesis of *Geopolitik*. Germany embarked upon a very successful policy in the *Schicksalsraum* and by the spring of 1941 was in control of most of what Haushofer had long before defined as being the eastern boundary lands of Europe, excepting only the three Baltic states and the eastern part of Poland.[52] While the Anti-Comintern Pact of 1936 had thus been a considerable setback for the strategy of *Geopolitik*, the Nazi-Soviet Pact both provided a tailor-made arrangement for securing the German domination of *Mitteleuropa* and was a reversion to the preferred geopolitical strategy for the penetration of the Heartland.

Then came the German invasion of the Soviet Union which must have been regarded by most of the *Geopolitiker*, none more than Haushofer himself, as a gross blunder, although *Zeitschrift* obediently changed tack and made the best of it. Geography had overnight been converted from ally to enemy, and this was coupled with the classic German nightmare of war on two fronts. Yet, despite the momentous decision which had been taken, there was at first astonishing success and within six months the whole of the extended *Kulturboden* was in the hands of the *Wehrmacht*. Maps appearing in *Zeitschrift* added this to the *Reichsgebiet* now extending from the Rhine to the Dnieper and from the Baltic Sea to the Danube. Then, from the winter of 1941–2 on, the physical environment was converted into the bitterest of enemies, and, as with Napoleon a century and a quarter before, Russia's ally, *le général février*, proved impossible for the *Wehrmacht* to defeat, although the war dragged on for a further three years. Just at the moment when the true magnitude of the potential eastern disaster was becoming evident, Hitler compounded this error with the even greater one of declaring war on the United States following the Japanese attack on Pearl Harbor.[53] The alliance of Germany with Japan having long been advocated, this in itself should not have displeased Haushofer. However, it ran very much counter to the notion of co-operation between the future German and American Pan-regions, and so was fundamentally against Germany's best interests. The extent to which this was so did not really become apparent until 1944.

Another important divergence between theory and practice was in the failure to establish control over the Mediterranean Sea. This was another strategic requirement which many *Geopolitiker* had considered to be an essential prerequisite to victory. Using her bases at Gibraltar, Malta, Cyprus and Suez, Britain succeeded in keeping this sea route open to allied shipping even during the worst times of the war when Malta was under constant bombardment and Axis submarines were operating around Gibraltar and Sicily. At the same time as keeping the route open to allied shipping, Britain had been able virtually to deny it to that of the enemy powers. Axis power in North Africa met with massive defeat at El Alamein in the autumn of 1942 and was completely eliminated by the allied forces in the summer of 1943. From then on, Hitler's European empire was under considerable pressure both from the south and from the east and with the construction of the Atlantic Wall, a kind of marine Maginot Line, the Third Reich was, after nearly seven years of aggressive expansion, at last forced onto the defensive. In the autumn of 1943, *Festung Europa* was invaded by sea through what Churchill had called its 'soft underbelly' and within a short time Italy had surrendered. This was the end of Mussolini's dream of *Mare Nostrum* and this appeared to vindicate the poor opinion held by the *Geopolitiker* of Italy's capacity to sustain the role of great power. The massive defeats suffered in 1943 in the Soviet Union and the Mediterranean were both sustained in the pursuit of policies which had been against the long-term advice of both Haushofer and many of his colleagues.

Even the actions of the Japanese were found to be wanting when measured against the advice given by Haushofer to the island empire. After the acquisition of Manchuria he had pointed out its geographical inadequacy as a potential colony and urged that Japan should rather turn her attention to the south. He felt the islands and peninsulas of South-East Asia to be a far more effective power-base and also more easily controlled and defended than was the Asian continent itself. The invasion of China proper in 1937 was also seen as an error, absorbing inordinate Japanese energy for very little return. His advice to Japan had been to make peace with the United States and so encourage the American giant to accept the South-East Asia Co-prosperity Sphere as he had hoped that she would accept Germany's New Order in Europe.

Even though after 1933 attempts were made to take on board Nazi ideas of racial superiority, there was always something of a contradiction between the idea of the *Herrenvolk* and that environmental determinism which was at the root of *Geopolitik*. Haushofer clearly became increasingly unhappy about this as the years wore on, the more so because such racialism was narrow and exclusive and its application made wider geopolitical aims more difficult to fulfil. The dichotomy was nowhere more clearly in evidence than in the aim of a united Europe led by Germany to which both the Nazis and the *Geopolitiker* aspired. It was official German policy after 1940 to encourage the peoples of the occupied countries to reach out from their petty nationalisms and to aspire rather towards a common destiny as Europeans. The war was presented in Nazi propaganda as a European crusade against external enemies, both to the west and to the east, whose alleged aim was to crush Europe out of existence. The whole nefarious operation was supposed to have been masterminded by the 'Jewish-Bolshevik conspiracy' which was deemed to be at the root of most of the world's evils. However, the grand European idea was doomed from the start by the brutal treatment accorded to non-Aryans, in particular those who had the misfortune to live in the occupied territories in the east. Jews, Slavs and many others were *Untermenschen* and as such they came at the very bottom of the New Order. Whatever was claimed to the contrary, it was soon evident from the actions of the German conquerors that the role of the other Europeans was to be that of workers or even slaves for the *Herrenvolk*. This led immediately to hostility and to the proliferation of underground resistance movements. In contrast to this, the *Geopolitiker* had advocated a policy of co-operation with the other Europeans and an attempt to move together towards the goal of a united, although German, Europe.

While perhaps the most momentous failure of the Nazis in Europe was their total inability to enlist the wholehearted support of the other peoples of the continent, on the world stage the dramatic collapse of the Thousand Year Reich was precipitated by the enmity of both the United States and the Soviet Union. While it was the Germans who actually declared war on them, both had independently been moving towards the conclusion that co-existence with the aggressive Central European state appeared to be virtually impossible. 'The costs of geographical ignorance are immensely high', said Haushofer when commenting on the apparent blindness of the British to world realities which to him appeared crystal clear. But the Germans, for all their alleged geo-graphical education, proved in the end to be no better at under-standing the implications of his *Geopolitik*. In 1942 Strausz-Hupé had asserted that *Geopolitik* had become Nazi foreign policy, but if this had ever been true it had certainly ceased to be so by then. The truth is that the strategy proposed by the *Institut für Geo-politik* was very different from the foreign policy actually pursued by the Nazis. Had the advice of the *Geopolitiker* been followed on such matters as the United States, the Mediterranean, European unity and the eastern lands, then Germany might even have won the war. Such was the nature of the Nazi hierarchy that it proved unreceptive to that kind of reasoned advice, for rational the Nazis most decidedly were not. While there is evidence that the con-ceptual framework of *Geopolitik* was used as a justification for conquest, there is little indication that many of the Nazi leaders were capable, either emotionally or intellectually, of appreciating the true significance of Haushofer's *Wissenschaft und Kunst.*

Whatever reservations the *Geopolitiker* may have had about the methods employed by their Nazi masters, they went along with them and inevitably they were themselves tarnished by the crimes perpetrated in the name of race and *Lebensraum*. In this respect they were very little different from all the others who had hovered like moths around the Nazi candle when it was shining most brightly. Inside Germany were the nationalists, aristocrats, industrialists, failed intellectuals and leaders of the *Wehrmacht*, and outside were Fascists, Vichy France, racists and hosts of Quislings from one end of Europe to the other. They all sought glory, or perhaps only safety, under the banner of the swastika. In the end all had chosen the wrong side and all were to be dragged down in the *Götterdämmerung* of the Third Reich. It was not, after all, to be the birth of a New Europe — at least not in this par-ticular way.

Looked at geopolitically, there is both a terrible splendour and a measure of poetic justice in the end of the Third Reich. It was a fundamental precept of *Geopolitik* that flux and change were constant features of the world scene. It accorded with its biological foundations that evolutionary struggle was inherent in it, and this in turn was also a feature of the German national spirit. In Strausz-Hupé's words: 'Mackinder's vision accorded only too well with the martial philosophy of world power or downfall which explains so much about German national pathology.' He observed that there was 'in Mackinder's dogma . . . just the kind of finality for which the Wagnerian mentality yearns. The impending struggle promised to be titanic; the goal — the domination of the Eurasian Heartland — was as challengingly remote as the far-off places towards which Wagner's heroes interminably travel'.[54] The Heartland came to be possessed of a transcendental quality in which its role as 'the mystical cradle of world conquerors' was uncritically accepted. In the eschatology of *Geopolitik* it was from here that the conquering power would emerge. There would then be a final titanic struggle between the Teutons, led by the Germans, and the other races. There was also the suggestion, especially from Haushofer himself, that this Armageddon was destined to take place in the East, in the 'Indo-Pacific space' and that then and there the power would emerge which would rule the world.

While *Geopolitik* had this futuristic vision, the Nazis themselves tended to look to the past. As Fest remarked: 'The salvation he [Hitler] wanted to bring about was always aimed at restoring something of the great nineteenth century.'[55] Whatever their ideas of the future may have been, the *Geopolitiker* also derived much of their mental equipment from the past. This is nowhere more apparent than in the importance accorded to the possession of *Raum* as the 'state-biological rule of life'. From Kjellén on, it was firmly believed that its acquisition was the panacea for almost all the nation's ills and was a means for effectively safeguarding its interests. Fest comments that Hitler, in his desire to 'justify his claims to *Lebensraum* reveals his inability to grasp modern solutions for exploiting what land is available'. In this fundamental respect, at least, the Nazis were very close to the teachings of Haushofer. Of course, the *Geopolitiker* had been by no means unique in holding such views, since the grabbing of ever more territory had been a feature of all late nineteenth century imperialism. The difference was that while Western geopolitical thinking, such as that of Mackinder, tended after World War I to move away from imperialism and towards a wider internationalism, the

84   *German* Geopolitik *and its Antecedents*

German *Geopolitiker* moved in just the opposite direction. In place of *sub specie aeternitatis* they substituted *sub specie Germaniae* and in so doing they firmly rejected all principles of universal applicability. Nazism has been seen as a revolt against Western civilisation by the Germanic tribes in their primeval forests; *Geopolitik* became in many ways the intellectual counterpart of this. It assumed the role of intellectual patron of the 'German spirit' and the justifier of its territorial expansion. The scholar's task was to 'prepare the way for the statesman by investigating the prerequisites of a just division of areas on our planet', said Haushofer. But, of course, they went much further than that and so their geographical philosophy was dragged down, along with most else, in the destruction which followed.

Notes

1. Quoted in S.D. Stirk, 'Myths, Types and Propaganda' in G.P. Gooch *et al.*, *The German Mind and Outlook* (Chapman and Hall, London, 1945).
2. The Rhineland was occupied by British, French and Belgian troops, and German forces were forbidden there.
3. Quoted in Stirk, 'Myths, Types and Propaganda'.
4. J. Partsch, *Central Europe* (Frowde, London, 1906).
5. F. Naumann, *Central Europe* (King, London, 1915).
6. O. Spengler, *The Decline of the West*, translated by C.F. Atkinson, (Allen and Unwin, London, 1922).
7. Stirk, 'Myths, Types and Propaganda'.
8. R. Kjellén, *Staten som Lifsform* (Stockholm, 1916, translated into German as *Der Staat als Lebensform* (Hirzel, Leipzig, 1917).
9. R. Kjellén, *Die Grossmacht der Gegenwart* (Teubner, Leipzig and Berlin, 1914).
10. Ibid.
11. D. Calleo, *The German Problem Reconsidered* (Cambridge University Press, Cambridge, 1978).
12. H.W. Weigert, *Generals and Geographers: The Twilight of Geopolitics* (Oxford University Press, New York, 1942).
13. A science and an art.
14. It is a duty to learn from the enemy.
15. K. Haushofer, *Weltpolitik von Heute* (Gerlag und Vertriebsgesellschaft, Berlin, 1936).
16. J. Fairgrieve, *Geographie und Weltmacht*, translated by M. Haushofer (Vowinckel, Berlin, 1925).
17. K. Haushofer, *Das Japanische Reich in seiner Geographischen Entwickelung* (Siedel, Vienna, 1921).
18. K. Haushofer, *Geopolitik des Pazifischen Ozeans* (Vowinckel, Berlin, 1924, revised edn 1938).
19. K. Haushofer, *Geopolitik der Panideen* (Vowinckel, Berlin, 1931).
20. Haushofer, *Weltpolitik von Heute.*
21. Seamanship is essential — another of Haushofer's favourite Latin

quotations.
22. K. Haushofer, *Zeitschrift für Geopolitik*, xii (1935).
23. W. Siewert, 'Die Geographischen Grundlagen der Deutschen Seestellung', *Zeitschrift für Geopolitik*, 10 (1933).
24. Haushofer, *Geopolitik der Panideen.*
25. K. Haushofer, 'The Call of the Sea' in A. Dorpalen, *The World of General Haushofer* (Farrar and Rinehart, New York, 1942).
26. J. März, 'Geopolitische Tagesarbeit', *Zeitschrift für Geopolitik*, 6 (1929).
27. K. Haushofer, *Grenzen in ihrer Geographischen und Politischen Bedeutung* (Vowinckel, Berlin, 1927, revised edn 1939).
28. Ibid.
29. R.E. Dickinson, *The German Lebensraum* (Penguin, Harmondsworth, 1943).
30. R.E. Heber, *Verfassung* (Hamburg, 1937).
31. J. Kühn, 'Über den Sinn des Gegenwärtigen Krieges', *Zeitschrift für Geopolitik*, 17 (1940).
32. K. Haushofer, 'Boundary Sense' in A. Dorpalen, *The World of General Haushofer.*
33. K. Haushofer, *Die Grossmacht vor und nach dem Weltkriege Deutschland* (Vowinckel, Berlin, 1930).
34. K. Haushofer, *Dai Nihon* (Mittler, Berlin, 1913).
35. The Treaty of Rapallo (1922) between Germany and the Soviet Union normalised relations and inaugurated a brief but fruitful period of co-operation between the two powers.
36. German-Soviet treaty of 1939 which gave Germany a free hand in the West and, in effect, divided Eastern Europe between the two powers.
37. K. Haushofer, 'Bericht über den Indopazifischen Raum', *Zeitschrift für Geopolitik*, 16 (1939).
38. R. Strausz-Hupé, *Geopolitics: The Struggle for Space and Power* (Putnam, New York, 1942).
39. The Treaty of Brest-Litovsk (March 1918) between Germany and Russia reduced the territory of Russia west of the Urals by a third and was a great diplomatic and military defeat for the new Soviet government.
40. A. Hitler, *Mein Kampf,* translated as *My Struggle* (Hurst and Blacket, London, 1933).
41. The Statute of Westminster (1931) clarified the status of the dominions as autonomous communities within the British Empire. It therefore institutionalised the centrifugal tendencies as the Empire began to give place to the idea of the Commonwealth.
42. K. Haushofer, 'Power and Space' in A. Dorpalen, *The World of General Haushofer.*
43. W. Pahl, *Das Politische Antlitz der Erde: ein Weltpolitischer Atlas* (Goldman, Leipzig, 1938).
44. K. Haushofer, 'Berichterstattung aus der Indopazifischen Welt', *Zeitschrift für Geopolitik*, i (1924).
45. Haushofer, *Geopolitik der Panideen.*
46. Haushofer, *Weltpolitik von Heute.*
47. The statement by President Monroe in 1823 that any attempt by European powers to extend their influence in the Americas would be regarded by the United States as constituting a danger to the peace of the whole of the Western Hemisphere.
48. A. Gyorgy, *Geopolitics: the New German Science* (University of California Press, Berkeley, 1944), Chapter XIV.
49. A. Benni, 'Italiens Wirtschaft und der Faschismus', *Zeitschrift für Geopolitik*, 6 (1929).

50. E. Fischer, 'The Passing of Mitteleuropa' in W.G. East and H.E. Moodie (eds.), *The Changing World* (Harrap, London, 1956).

51. Strausz-Hupé, *Geopolitics: The Struggle for Space and Power.*

52. All these territories, together with Bessarabia and Northern Bukovina had been allocated to the Soviet sphere by the secret clauses of the Nazi-Soviet Pact.

53. This attack took place in December 1941 and was followed rather than preceded by a Japanese declaration of war on the United States. From then on all the major belligerents were engaged and the battle lines were drawn.

54. Ibid.

55. J.C. Fest, *Hitler* (Weidenfeld and Nicolson, London, 1974) Book 8 Chapter 2.

6 L'ESPRIT VIDALIENNE VERSUS GEOPOLITIK: FRENCH GEOPOLITICAL THOUGHT BEFORE WORLD WAR II

There was not in France a tradition of the study of political geography in any way comparable to that in Germany. Paul Vidal de la Blache, the doyen of French geography, had died in 1918 just before the end of World War I. It was he who had given the French school its particular character, and *la tradition vidalienne* was to remain central to French geography throughout the inter-war period. This emphasised the concept of geography as a science unifying all terrestrial phenomena, its highest expression being regional synthesis. Vidal had himself considered that *la géographie politique* could not properly be studied without reference to the whole body of human geography since he saw it essentially as a part of the totality. However, it was rapidly realised that in the post-war world international relations were going to play a crucial role, and that geographers needed to be aware of this. Following the signature of the Treaty of Versailles, Lucien Gallois observed: 'It will be necessary to give attention to the study of states and the political organisations which these arrangements are going to create.'[1] As the years passed, such attention was certainly given, particularly as the European situation began to deteriorate in the late 1920s and apprehension in France began to grow. The French geographers soon became aware of Karl Haushofer and his *Geopolitik*, and of its dire implications for the future of France as a great power. It was against this forbidding backcloth that French geopolitical thinking was formulated.

The initial preoccupation of the *Geopolitiker* had been with Britain and Russia, the two antagonistic world powers in the Mackinder-Haushofer *Weltanschauung*. Together they stood accused of having deprived Germany of her geopolitical freedom of action, and in alliance they were considered quite capable of crushing Mitteleuropa out of existence. Of the two, Britain was seen as being the more dangerous to Germany, but before British power could be confronted and destroyed it was necessary to dispose of France. This was both because France lay between Germany and the ocean and because *la grande nation* herself possessed hegemonial aspirations in Europe incompatible with those of Germany. She was regarded as the traditional enemy, the main opponent of German expansion in *Mitteleuropa* and the principal architect and guarantor of the hated *Teufelsgürtel* (Figure 5.5). She had been the centre and heart of the alliance which had encircled and defeated Germany in World War I, and since 1918, adding insult to injury, had returned to the left bank of the Rhine. The demilitarisation of the Rhineland meant that while German troops were banned, the French for a time had troops in the Ruhr and elsewhere. Since the Rhine was regarded by the Germans as being *'Deutschlands Strom aber nicht Deutschlands Grenze'*,[2] while to the French it was a part of their *'limites naturelles'*, the whole matter had become a very emotional one on both sides.[3]

In view of all this, it might appear surprising that so little attention was given to France in the *Zeitschrift für Geopolitik* as compared to that given to Britain, the United States and the Far East. This is explained by the fact that the *Geopolitiker* saw France as being a power in a state of decline, since she had expended her resources in too profligate a manner. The geographical problem running through French history was that she had both a continental and an oceanic front and had divided her limited energies between them. 'France's history shows curious changes from continental to oceanic tendencies and back again,' said Haushofer, but he concluded that France, like Germany, did not really understand the importance of the sea and that continental considerations had invariably taken precedence over oceanic ones.[4]

Then there was France's demographic weakness arising from her historically low birth-rates. The consequence of this was that she was a relatively lightly populated country, in contrast to the very high densities of Germany whose population had increased so fast after 1871. Furthermore, they saw the 'bastardisation' of the French race arising from the country's colonial associations. It was now, according to Haushofer, a half-African state, and an inefficient one at that. The French were compared unfavourably with the British as a colonial people and were classed with the Portuguese and the Spaniards. Hennig accused them of using 'Carthaginian methods' in pillaging their colonial territories but not developing them, and of sacrificing the subject peoples to French interests.[5] They were grouped in the ranks of those 'space robbers' with territories too large for them to control and digest. Dix claimed: 'France as a world power is finished. The days of French colonial policy are numbered. A great part of its empire finds itself exposed to the twin dangers of Islam and nationalism.'[6] There was clearly a good deal of contempt for this decadent nation, stagnating behind the Maginot line and doomed to be eliminated as a great power in the coming struggle with the far more dynamic, fecund and powerful Germany. Haushofer envisaged presciently a *Blitzkrieg* against France which would enable Germany to establish domination over Europe before intervention could take place from either west or east. Ultimately it would be necessary to persuade France to throw in her lot with Germany in the creation of the New Order, but this would not be accomplished until France was convinced that she could not hope for an alliance with either of the great continental or oceanic powers.

The French political geographers viewed this scenario as being based on the ideas of Ratzel and his disciples, and they therefore attacked it at source, namely the anthropomorphic conception of the state and the iron laws of geopolitical influences on it. Most of the assertions of the *Geopolitiker* were regarded as being spurious, none more so than the implied belief in German superiority and the inevitability of European hegemony for the so-called Aryan peoples. It was dismissed by Goblet as 'pseudo-scientific geographical determinism and false ideas of race' and he concluded that 'some learned pedant is always to be found to demonstrate that the terrestrial appetites of the state are absolutely justified, and that from the natural order of things, if not from God himself, they derive a sacred character'.[7] The endowment of the state with such metaphysical attributes came in for particular attack and ridicule, and this is central to the rejection of the claims of *Geopolitik* to be really scientific. Goblet concluded that it had become the agent of a sort of 'state mysticism' and fed on just the sort of nationalistic sentiments which had led to war in 1914. He went on to suggest that such German ideas as these had been profoundly influenced by Hebrew religious thought. 'Mysticism became the handmaiden of the German will to power ... The earth was the foundation of this castle of dreams; it was clothed in the guise of 'natural' territory, destined for the chosen people, who were the Germans.'[8]

The French political geographers found all this quite impossible to swallow. Setting such store as they did on precise observation and interpretation, its aggregate effect on them, despite its apparently authentic scientific clothing, was, in Siegfried's phrase to cause '*la nausée*'. To Febvre it was 'worthless glitter', and in spite of the invocation of great world systems he felt that in the end nothing whatsoever was really very satisfactorily explained. To him it appeared to be little more than the continued chanting of the 'old Ratzelian litanies'.[9] The fact that, in any case, France was destined to play so small and ignominious a role in them also gave rise to a profound disquiet which underlay the other reasons for the hostility of the French geographers.

In contrast to the materialist inevitability which weighed down *Geopolitik*, *l'esprit vidalienne* proclaimed the triumph of humanity, and of human civilisation, in its relationship with its physical environment. This latter always contained many possibilities and it was up to man himself to make the right choices. Man was perceived as being a positive rather than a negative agent in his relationship to the physical world. As Febvre put it with a touch of irony: 'Between man and his natural environment ideas are always creeping in and intervening.' The belief in *élan*, founded on free will, made the materialistic soullessness of *Geopolitik* quite unacceptable. It did not allow for that Bergsonian vitalism which was so much a part of the French intellectual tradition, and it was on this that the French political geographers based their own particular interpretations of the world.

It was not only the ideology of *Geopolitik* which alarmed the French geographers, but also the country which had given birth to it. As Demangeon said: 'Of all the national states grown recently on the soil of old Europe there exists none more original, nor more disquieting, than Germany.'[10] Ancel saw Germany as a political mass which weighed down heavily on Central Europe, a region which came to be regarded as being fraught with considerable menace. To de Martonne *Mitteleuropa* (*l'Europe centrale*) was 'a land of prolonged political instability, responding to an ethnic instability, a meeting place of influences which come together more harmoniously in oceanic Europe and which are spread out more widely to the east in continental Europe'.[11] Zimmermann in his review of de Martonne's book in *Annales de Géographie* emphasised both the interior and exterior tensions which had made Central Europe into 'a sort of cauldron in which the elements have not yet succeeded in fusing themselves into a fixed alloy'.[12]

There was then widespread condemnation by French political geographers of what they regarded as being the 'pseudo-geography' across the Rhine and alarm at the rebirth of Germany and the dangers which this posed for their own country. However, there was little general agreement on an alternative geopolitical philosophy for the age. They ranged widely and covered a great variety of regions and subjects, but the ones which keep recurring most frequently relate to Europe, maritime imperialism and the rapidity of developments in other parts of the world.

Demangeon contended in 1920 that since the beginning of the twentieth century, Europe had been losing the world hegemony which it had built up over the previous two centuries.[13] He saw the main beneficiaries of European decline as being the United States of America and Japan. As he put it: 'The unity of the world was brought into being on a European model; there is no longer unity but a plurality of influences.' 'Europe is no longer a driving force in the world,' wrote Siegfried on the same theme in 1927, and he saw the European world system as doomed to disappear in face of the great world forces then ranging against it.[14] The question of the *malaise* from which the old Europe appeared to be suffering was subsequently taken up in a number of articles in *Annales de Géographie.* These largely accepted the thesis that Europe was decadent and that America and Japan were together the principal inheritors of its world role. They were, in the view of Decugis, the forerunners of a wider emancipation of the colonial peoples and as this happened he saw what he called 'the equilibrium of world forces' being destroyed. A spatial manifestation of European decadence is seen by Decugis as being the break-up of larger political units and the proliferation of small independent states: 'The centrifugal tendencies which push towards disunion and dismemberment are now much stronger than the tendencies to agglomeration and confederation.'[15] Ferenczi talked of the 'cyclic evolution of nations' and saw the manifest decline of the European powers being reflected in their low birth-rates. In contrast to this, birth-rates in the newer nations were much higher.[16]

The principal geopolitical manifestation of the European global hegemony was maritime imperialism, and there appeared to be widespread agreement among French political geographers that the British Empire was the finest example of this. In *L'Empire Britannique*[17] Demangeon stated categorically that 'Europe faces the other peoples of the world with an Anglo-Saxon front' provided by 'the richest and most populous colonial empire that the world has ever seen'. He saw its lifeline as being the sea, the common bond without which the empire would be reduced to merely 'a dust of islands' spread over the globe. Its historic role was the development of the rest of the world after the European model, 'to break down those forces of inertia which hold it bound, and to inoculate its organism with the vital ferments prepared in the hothouses of Europe'. Although after World War I the Empire was larger than ever before, already in 1923 Demangeon saw that it faced great problems in the new post-war world. The most important of these were distance, heterogeneity and ubiquity, all three being forces for disintegration. He singled out Islam as being a focus of danger both to the British Empire and to the other European empires: 'It appears that a certain solidarity is tending to be established between all peoples who feel themselves to be strangers to European civilisation, and nowhere does this solidarity appear so close as in the Muslim world.' He observed that Islam was rising once more as a political power just as the prestige of Britain in the East was diminishing.

Goblet, writing over a decade later, saw the centre of the British Empire as having moved to India and the Indian Ocean and he pointed out the crucial significance of the route to the East via the Suez canal.[18] This was the 'imperial British' routeway, but it also had the wider function of connecting the thalassocracies of Western Europe with their colonies in the East. Although Britannia was still holding 'the trident of Poseidon' the empire was in course of evolution and its dependencies were becoming stronger and more important at the expense of the mother country. This evolution, speculated Goblet, could signify the Empire's coming end, but 'this power possesses a wonderful faculty of adaptation, which constitutes its greatness and may assure its permanence'. Ancel, writing just before the outbreak of World War II saw the British Commonwealth as still defying distance and braving ubiquity, but increasingly under threat from new spiritual ideals.[19] He saw the old imperial ideal as being no match for the rising tide of idealistic nationalism, especially in India, the heart of the Empire. Febvre saw the fragility of the European world systems as compared to the far greater strength of 'the natural regions of the great states' such as Islam, India and the Far East.[20] These *mondes* he considered to be the true political, intellectual and moral consolidations of power and realities of great world significance for the future.

In face of this spectacle of all too evident European decline, both internally and globally, most of the French political geographers took a remarkably indulgent and understanding view of the imperial expansion of both America and Japan. As Goblet said: 'There is no more break of continuity between Florida and Puerto Rico than there is between Pennsylvania and Florida. The interdependence between tropical America and the North American continent explains what is called American imperialism.' This complementarity is 'in accordance with the natural order of things'. He saw the Japanese conquests of Korea and Manchuria in much the same light and even anticipated a Japanese move into Mongolia where she would confront the Soviet Union over the mountains of Central Asia. 'It is singularly childish to "denounce" all this as "imperialism" and to oppose old juridical texts to these manifestations of life. A whole Japanese world is in course of organisation, based upon natural interdependence.'[21] Manchuria, in Ancel's view, was a natural colony of a dynamic Japan seeking land for its overcrowded insular population. It is significant that Goblet in particular laid stress on the natural and organic character of what was happening as the world moved towards a state of stable equilibrium. He warned that 'politico-geographical organisms ... cannot be mutilated with impunity'.

Besides this, there was a great interest in the Pacific theatre and a predisposition to regard it as being the geopolitical region of the future. Demangeon in 1923 had quoted Smuts' assertion that the centre of gravity of British imperial politics was moving towards the Far East and the Pacific. Decugis saw the advantage swinging towards the immense Asiatic masses and he believed that, organised by Japan, Asia was capable of becoming the economic centre of the world. Goblet also emphasised the role of Japan as the hegemonial power of the whole Far Eastern region: 'The history of the Philippines seems to be entering upon a new phase when the archipelago will become more and more closely associated with the geographical and human environment in which Nature placed it: an environment lit by the rays of the Rising Sun.' He saw the Pacific becoming a 'marchland' and a meeting place of the opposing empires of the 'Far West' and the 'Far East', the latter clearly dominated by the 'Rising Sun'.[22] To Siegfried America was becoming increasingly a Pacific power, and he saw the west coast as a world frontier with the Far East. He refers to the Asiatic masses as being the 'Yellow Peril', a danger to the security of the other peoples of the region. He contemplates the rise of a 'new constellation' of power in the Pacific with America replacing Britain in the role of leader and protector of the white races there.[23]

How did the French political geographers see their own country's place in these panoramas of world geopolitical evolution? It was agreed almost unanimously that the most pressing problem was that of her aggressive and unstable eastern neighbour. The French geographers countered the German concepts of *Mitteleuropa* and *Deutscher Kulturboden* with their own concepts of *élan* and *civilisation* in *la tradition vidalienne*. 'The geopolitical idea of space (*Raum*) clashes with the Western idea of cooperation (*groupement*),' said Ancel.[24] It is the association of *pays* with their particular *genres de vie* which eventually produces nationality. This arises from the wider conditions of the environment of which man forms a part, and in the creation of which he plays an active role. The ancient *civilisation rhénane* had evolved and flourished in its natural evironment and had lasted until destroyed by the enforced Prussianisation (*Musspreussen*) of the nineteenth century which Ancel labelled the *Anschluss rhénan*. Out of this had been born the idea of the *Deutsches Rhein* with German, that is to say Prussian, dominance. Ancel countered this with the concept of the *frontière spirituelle* delimiting a people rather than a territory, but a people which feels itself to be a nation and desires to remain so. He invoked the ideals of the French Revolution and the concepts of nationality and of frontiers which were then formulated. Alongside this there was Vidal's *esprit frontalière* in which a people know themselves the better for a knowledge of others and of the real cultural differences which divide them. '*Le moi prend conscience du lui-même au contact du non-moi*' was his famous phrase. The traditional French idea of *les limites naturelles* of which the Rhine was one was also criticised by both Febvre and Ancel. Frontiers must not be considered as being immutable or fixed by destiny but as being liable to change, and such changes had to be based upon new geographical realities. Ancel warns that 'geography will take its revenge' on those who would ignore them purely for reasons of power.

In opposition to the 'watertight bulkheads' produced by the Nazi policy of national autarchy, the French geographers advocated a permeability of frontiers based on international co-operation. The whole of Europe would benefit from such a development. Great civilisations have arisen in open societies and not in those which habitually hide behind high walls. Demangeon translated this idea into an appeal for the settlement of problems on an international level, and for an united Europe, of which he hoped that Great Britain would form an integral part.[25] Already in 1928 he suggested that Britain was torn between conflicting pressures emanating from Europe and from the Empire and that she would have to choose between them. Ferenczi concluded that for a Europe in decline co-operation was a far more appropriate response than confrontation.[26]

Underlying the scholarly and analytic approach of the French there was an appreciation of the very real weakness of France, and in particular of her vulnerability in face of her powerful eastern neighbour. Thus a united Europe, and one of which Britain, her principal ally, formed a part was very much in the international interests of France. French language and culture still retained their pre-eminence from the Channel to the Baltic and the Black Sea, and it was this aspect of international influence, rather than the recourse to brute force, which had the greater appeal to French scholars.

A second method of improving the position of France was seen to be through the development of her colonial empire. This had become a major national preoccupation since the end of the nine-teenth century and a growing proportion of the nation's human and physical resources were spent on it. However, its importance to the country's political and military leadership was far from being reflected in the attention given to it by French political geo-graphers. Far more admiration was lavished on the British Empire as the supreme example of its kind than on the smaller and more modest home product. It was Great Britain which had been the leader of the white race across the world, according to Siegfried, and 'even French activities in Africa were of only secondary importance'.[27] Demangeon in *Le Déclin de l'Europe* saw the necessity for France to work very hard to maintain her position in a world of competing great powers and urged the association of the colonies with this enterprise. Only in this way could the chronic imbalance between France and Germany be redressed since it was the only respect in which France was now better off than Germany.

The colonial empire was also seen in the role of potential rejuvenator of *la vieille France* itself. Demangeon considered a nation to be fortunate which possessed a *front de colonisation* since it produced a vitality in the frontiersmen subjected as they were to the struggle against the rigours of nature on the edges of the desert, the steppe and the forest. 'As the frontier of colonisation advances, so the nation itself progresses and is enriched,' said Demangeon,[28] but he was clearly disappointed at the slowness of the French colonial advance in North Africa as compared to that of the British in their territories. Hardy[29] and Ferenczi were also enthusiastic about the merits of colonial development, although the latter pointed to the adverse effects on colonialism of the slowing down of the European birth-rates. Ancel, preoccupied with European affairs, was far less enthusiastic about it. He spoke of the French in the Maghreb as but the latest in a succession of imperial peoples which had occupied this island between the sea and the sand and had never really come to terms with it. Grouping the French alongside the Romans, Byzantines and Ottomans, he implies, with some prescience, that despite the current enthusiasms, their fate eventually would be much the same.[30] By implication geography would take its revenge as much on French ambitions in Africa as on Prussian ambitions in the Rhinelands.

One senses that, although naturally more predisposed to scholarly monographs, the French were forced into macro-geopolitical thinking by the increasing menace of the international situation. The amount of writing on politico-geographic topics increased substantially throughout the inter-war period and particularly during the five years before the outbreak of World War II.

Their response may be summarised as having been to present fundamental alternatives to power politics and to the use of physical force in achieving ends. The merits of *civilisation* were presented in contrast to those of *Kultur*; spiritual power against *Macht*; man the active agent against blind environmentalism, and international co-operation against nationalistic autarchy. There should be open frontiers rather than closed ones, and close observation and realism in place of abstraction and the pursuit of universal laws. In summary, it was a humanistic as opposed to a theological approach. There was little attempt by the French geographers to oppose German territorial claims with counter-claims of a similar order. Rather they proposed radical alternatives to the thinking on the other side of the Rhine. The French geographers were naturally more aware than most of their fellow countrymen of the very real weakness of France, and the broad intellectual front on which they confronted the Germans may therefore also have been judged to be the most realistic way in which French interests could most effectively be pursued.

Nevertheless, there were some surprising similarities between the ideas of French political geographers, particularly in the late 1930s, and their German counterparts. Both stressed the decadence of Europe and the loss of its hegemonial position in relation to the rest of the world. Both also saw the answer, in part at least, in a united Europe, but each had in mind something quite different. They were agreed on the significance of the rise of the United States and Japan and the threat which both these powers posed to Europe's world position. The great European empires, in particular the British, looked as though they were coming to an end, but while for the *Geopolitiker* this was cause for rejoicing, for the French there was little joy in it, partly because they were imperialists too and were thus part of the decline. For Haushofer, as for Goblet, the Pacific was the region of the future, and it was there that a massive confrontation appeared likely, even 'destined', to take place. For both Goblet and Ancel, as for the *Geopolitiker*, frontiers were not to be regarded as there *ad aeternam*, but as being political isobars. Necessary evolutionary change, in accordance with altered circumstances, had to be accepted. This ranged them together against the static, or at least arthritic, notions of the pre-war European order and the equal rigidity of the League of Nations world system.

However, despite such resemblances, it was the profound differences between the two which really counted. While both saw signs that the disorder of the times was indicative of a new world system coming into being, to the French this should be based on the principles of internationalism, while to the Germans it was to be a new form of continental imperialism. Ultimately French political geography at this time was about securing peace and not about making war. It was about how, through achieving a better understanding of geopolitical reality, the world's problems could be more effectively dealt with. It was about using the light of creative intelligence to illuminate the dark corners of the world. In this it remained firmly in the *vidalien* tradition, and was far removed in spirit from that Wagnerian world across the Rhine.

The major international preoccupation of the French politicians, both at Versailles and during the inter-war period, was security in Europe. The fear of Germany was soon to re-emerge after 1918, and the consciousness of France's economic and demographic weakness as compared with her powerful eastern neighbour cast a shadow over the period. It produced a defensive psychology which was nowhere more in evidence than in military strategy. The central problem was seen as being the vulnerability of the French hexagon in face of attack from the east, and particularly the dangers of the 'invasion corridor' through Belgium. The geographical expression of this static mentality was the Maginot Line, the apotheosis of the trenches of World War I, initially intended for the defence of the regained but still highly vulnerable eastern provinces of Alsace and Lorraine. It was expressed politically in the attempt to construct a system of alliances with the new countries of Eastern Europe. This *cordon sanitaire*, or at least parts of it, thus replaced Russia as the ally in the East and was the focus of French endeavours to force any aggressive new German state to face the hated prospect of war on two fronts. After 1933 the Third Reich soon began to flex its muscles and to break out of the tight girdle which France had attempted to put around it. Stages in this process between 1935 and 1938 were the return of the Saarland, the remilitarisation of the Rhineland, the *Anschluss* with Austria and the acquisition of the Sudetenland from Czechoslovakia. These menacing developments initially produced little response in France, and alongside her ally Great Britain she connived at the dismemberment of Czechoslovakia. 'Why should we care if three million Germans want to be German?' was the reaction of the French satirical journal *Le Canard Enchaîné*. In deference to Belgian susceptibilities, even the much vaunted Maginot Line was not extended on to the coast. When war came in 1939 defeat was already in the air and, following the unnerving phoney war — the *drôle de guerre* — the military collapse in June was terrible in its swiftness. The Battle of France was lost, according to Denis Brogan, because it was fought between Frenchmen and Frenchmen.[31]

In France as in Germany, geography was an established subject in schools and universities and most educated Frenchmen of the time would have been familiar with basic geographical thinking. Clemenceau himself had been well aware in 1918 that the satisfaction of French security requirements had to be based upon an appreciation of the realities of European geography. However France did not produce a Mackinder or a Fairgrieve to put this into a wider geopolitical perspective. As has been observed, the French political geographers of the inter-war period took a broadly humanist perspective. They were very much in the camp of those who upheld all that the French labelled *civilisation* and they were consequently disinclined to address themselves to the issues of war and strategy. Political geography, said Goblet in 1935, was 'above all other sciences a work of peace'. Its field was concrete reality and so it demonstrated 'the emptiness of mystical nationalism'.

Despite this, the whole concept of *les limites naturelles* was essentially a geopolitical one and it underpinned the French strategic thinking of the time. Generations of French schoolchildren had been taught the geography of France as though there was something almost mathematically inevitable about its particular morphology. The outlines of France had been drawn by its geography, according to Albert Sorel.[32] Hence the anguish when the sacred hexagon was tampered with in 1871 and the unbridled joy when it was given back its correct geometry in 1918.[33] The Maginot Line was a physical expression both of this static approach and of the deep fear and antipathy felt towards Germany. Charles de Gaulle, writing in 1924, had subscribed to the notion of the age-old rivalry between '*Gaullois et Germains*' and asserted that 'wherever it passes, the French-German frontier is the lip of the wound'.[34] Yet de Gaulle's military thinking was dynamic rather than static in its approach, and it was consequently to prove more influential in Germany than in France. He inadvertently helped Guderian and others to refine their thinking on the future role of tank warfare and *Blitzkrieg*. De Gaulle was referred to in *Zeitschrift* as being one of those Frenchmen who resisted the country's steady decline and attempted to defend its position in Europe. It was the knowledge that this type of thinking existed in France which made the *Geopolitiker* refrain from writing the country off entirely.

In fact most of the French political geographers were hostile both to the concept of *les limites naturelles* and of frontiers as 'watertight bulkheads'. Vauban, in Ancel's view had 'surrounded the kingdom with a stone corselet' in an attempt to make its frontiers eternal. This, he maintained, was neither desirable nor realistic since there must be movement in man as in nature. In place of the *barrière rigoureuse* he substituted a *périphérie toujours provisoire.* After World War II Jean Gottmann accused Ancel of having made a bad attempt at compromise between French and German thinking. Yet in the late 1930s Ancel had been an implacable opponent both of *Geopolitik* and of *prussianisme.* He fell foul of the occupiers of his country and died in a German concentration camp in 1942.

Demangeon, also an outspoken critic of *Geopolitik* died in the early months of the occupation. He had continued to believe strongly in the necessity for Europe to unite in face of developments taking place in other parts of the world. Demangeon's ideas on this subject were well known to the French political leader Aristide Briand, who during the 1920s had fought vigorously for Franco-German reconciliation. He promoted the idea of a United States of Europe and was supported in this by Gustav Stresemann, Foreign Minister in Germany's Weimar Republic. The premature death of Stresemann in 1929 and the ascendancy of the Nazi party afterwards put paid to internationalist ideas of this sort. The Briand Plan of 1930 was nevertheless a forerunner of the European Community idea originated by Jean Monnet and supported by Robert Schuman after World War II.[35]

France fell in June 1940 after only six weeks of fighting and that twilight which had been foreseen by Goblet five years earlier was followed by the long night of the German occupation. Some French geographers left and found refuge in the Anglo-Saxon countries. Jean Gottmann went to America where in 1942 he became geographical consultant at the Board of Economic Warfare in Washington. French political geography came to an abrupt end and did not emerge again until years after the end of the war. By that time the Americans had become the principal torchbearers of the geopolitical traditions of the West.

Notes

1. L. Gallois, 'La Paix de Versailles: les nouvelles frontières de l'Allemagne', *Annales de Géographie*, XXVIII, 154 (1919).

2. Germany's river but not Germany's frontier (from a poem by J. Arndt, written in 1813).

3. G. Parker, *A Political Geography of Community Europe* (Butterworth, London, 1983), Chapter 4, note 9.

4. K. Haushofer, *Zeitschrift für Geopolitik*, 12 (1935).

5. A. Demangeon, 'La Géographie Politique', *Annales de Géographie*, XLI, 229 (1932).

6. Ibid.

7. Y.M. Goblet, *The Twilight of Treaties* (Bell, London, 1936), Chapter II.

8. Ibid.

9. L. Febvre, *A Geographical Introduction to History* (Kegan Paul, Trench and Traubner, London, 1932), Chapter II.

10. A. Demangeon, 'Géographie Politique, à propos de l'Allemagne', *Annales de Géographie*, XLVIII, 272, (1939).

11. E. de Martonne, *L'Europe Centrale*, Géographie Universelle series (Armand Colin, Paris, 1931).

12. M. Zimmermann, 'Review of de Martonne, *L'Europe Centrale*', *Annales de Géographie*, XLII, 239 (1933).

13. A. Demangeon, *Le Déclin de l'Europe* (Payot, Paris, 1920).

14. A. Siegfried, *America Comes of Age* (London, 1927).

15. H. Decugis, *Le Destin des Races Blanches* (Librairie de France, Paris, 1936).

16. I. Ferenczi, 'La population blanche dans les colonies', *Annales de Géographie*, XLVII, 267 (1938).

17. A. Demangeon, 'Problèmes britanniques', *Annales de Géographie*, XXXI, 169 (1922); and *The British Empire: A Study in Colonial Geography* (Harrap, London, 1925).

18. Y.M. Goblet, *The Twilight of Treaties*.

19. J. Ancel, *Géographie des Frontières* (Gallimard, Paris, 1938).

20. L. Febvre, *A Geographical Introduction to History*.

21. Y.M. Goblet, *The Twilight of Treaties*.

22. Ibid.

23. A. Siegfried, *America Comes of Age*.

24. J. Ancel, *Géographie des Frontières*.

25. A. Demangeon, *The British Isles* (Heinemann, London, 1939) Chapters III and IV.

26. I. Ferenczi, 'La population blanche dans les colonies'.

27. A. Siegfried, *America Comes of Age*.

28. A. Demangeon, 'Pionniers et fronts de colonisation', *Annales de Géographie*, XLI, 233 (1932).

29. G. Hardy, *Géographie et Colonisation* (Paris, 1933).

30. J. Ancel, *Géographie des Frontières*.

31. D.W. Brogan, *The Development of Modern France: 1870-1939* (Hamish Hamilton, London, 1940).

32. N.J.G. Pounds, 'The Origin of the Idea of Natural Frontiers in France', *Annals of the Association of American Geographers*, 41 (1951).

33. G. Parker, *A Political Geography of Community Europe*, Chapter 4, Note 9.

34. C. de Gaulle, *La discorde chez l'ennemie* (Paris, 1924).

35. G. Parker, *A Political Geography of Community Europe*, Chapter 1.

7 BRAVE NEW GEOPOLITICS: THE DEVELOPMENT OF GEOPOLITICAL THOUGHT IN NORTH AMERICA

'The America of today is tired and old,' asserted Colin Ross, self-proclaimed specialist in the *Geopolitik* of the New World, writing in 1939, and he contrasted this with the new energy and dynamism he saw in Europe.[1] Like so many of Ross's judgements, this soon proved to be very wide of the mark. However, while the *Geopolitiker* so underestimated the potential of the great power across the Atlantic, the Americans made no such mistake about the significance of what was happening in Europe. American political geographers took up the study of *Geopolitik* with considerable enthusiasm. 'Geopolitics has migrated from Germany to America,' said Isaiah Bowman in 1942 just as a substantial literature on the subject was beginning to build up.[2] It was also taken up by the more popular magazines such as *Fortune* which produced articles on international events illustrated by explanatory maps. Under the influence of such factors, the whole subject for a time became something of a national fascination. It was the age of 'barbershop geopolitics' and M. Tagoff in a poem in the *New Yorker* commented:

> Ah blessed styptic on the nicks!
> O brave new geopolitics.[3]

The nature and aims of the magic new German 'super-science' were given considerable airing everywhere from the newspapers to the learned journals. Karl Haushofer, with his cohorts of 'scientists' in tow, was pictured as being the evil genius behind Hitler. It was even suggested that this shadowy figure was in reality the most important man in the Third Reich, virtually dictating the policies which Hitler then obediently followed.

While the political geographers rose to the occasion and produced a considerable literature on the subject, there was among the American people a widespread lack of the intellectual equipment with which to formulate an intelligent world view. The geographical knowledge of even well-educated Americans was for the most part quite superficial and old-fashioned. Before that time Americans, having been largely isolated from the rest of the world, had just not been that interested in world events. In the atmosphere of isolationism during the inter-war period they had, as Spykman put it, turned their gaze inward and in so doing had developed 'a strange provincialism'.[4] According to Archibald Coolidge the average American in 1898 could not have said whether Philippines was the name of an archipelago or the name of a jam, and the psychological climate had not changed a great deal in the intervening 40 years. 'Global geography was simply not in our blood,' lamented Hans Weigert.[5]

It was this state of ignorance which the political geographers of the 1940s set about rectifying. Besides books and articles, this entailed producing a new generation of explanatory maps, using new techniques and unfamiliar projections, in order to clarify the features of the world situation and of the background against which it was unfolding. It entailed sweeping away what Weigert called 'yesterday's geography', in so doing 'letting us see the world in the mirror of dynamic maps, instead of the static maps of times past'.[6] The ignorance which had encouraged the 'myth and magic' aspect of *Geopolitik* would then give place to a better understanding of what it was really all about and so of what America could do about it.

At this time interpretive books on German *Geopolitik* were written by Robert Strausz-Hupé,[7] Derwent Whittlesey,[8] and Andrew Gyorgy.[9] Andreas Dorpalen published extracts, translated into English, from the works of Karl Haushofer and other members of the Munich Institute.[10] There also appeared the beginnings of the formulation of an alternative global view which then continued to evolve throughout the 1940s. It was founded on the geopolitical ideas of the 1930s, but now the pace had intensified and the whole scope widened. The formulation of this 'new American *Weltanschauung* of global scope' is particularly identified with the names of Hans Weigert, Nicholas Spykman, Vilhjalmur Stefansson, Owen Lattimore and Derwent Whittlesey. Many others made significant, if more limited, contributions. Weigert encapsulated the aim by the use of one of Haushofer's favourite Latin quotations, *fas est ab hoste doceri* (see page 84, Note 14). The knowledge so gained about the nature of *Geopolitik* could then be used to create what he called a 'humanised geopolitics' which America could turn to her own needs. This would supply a dose of 'the badly needed vitamins' which would enable America to comprehend more clearly the nature of the world situation.

Perhaps the most fundamental aspect of the process of relearning the world's geography was the appreciation of the fact that the world was not flat but spherical, and of the implications of this for the relationships of the continents. Weigert regarded the Mercator projection as having been virtually a secret ally of Hitler and felt that it had held the geographical thought processes in its iron grip. It was high time, he thought, that 'the chains of Mercator' were broken so that global realities could be more fully appreciated and understood.[11] The Mercator world, traditionally emphasising the centrality of Europe, had relegated America to the sidelines, and in so doing had contributed to the spirit of isolationism in the United States. In addressing themselves to this situation, the American political geographers used alternative projections in an innovative manner. One such was the polar azimuthal equidistant which showed the dispositions of the northern land masses from quite an unfamiliar angle. It was particularly revealing in demonstrating the unfamiliar relationship between North America and Asia. It also demonstrated the concentration of the land masses in the Northern Hemisphere, reaching their greatest extent in mid-latitudes, and then tapering off, with 'starfishlike dispersion' as Spykman put it, towards the Southern Hemisphere. Harrison and Weigert showed how Mackinder's famous 'Pivot' map of 1904 gave a more revealing picture of the relationship of the Heartland to the other continents when transposed from Mercator to an azimuthal equidistant projection (Figure 7.1).

A fuller appreciation of the significance of such relationships was regarded as being of particular importance at the dawn of the age of air communication. As Stefansson said: 'The aviators found the world a cylinder but they left it a sphere.'[12] Now the fact that the earth was a sphere 'surrounded by a navigable ocean of air several miles deep' was of crucial importance. Mankind was seen as being on the verge of liberation from the physical obstacles which had always impeded his movement on the surface of the earth. Now with great circle routes following the shortest distances, the earth would achieve its 'final image' — that of the completed sphere.

A major change arising from this concerned the relative importance of the Arctic regions. Traditional world geography was turned upside down and these regions now became potentially

Figure 7.1: Mackinder's Pivot Transposed from Mercator to Azimuthal Projection

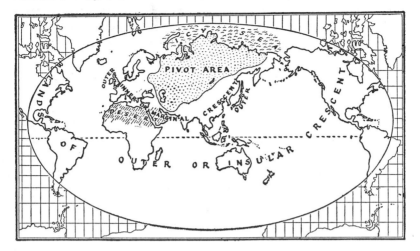

(a) The famous Mackinder oval map extended out to the rectangle of the mercator projection.

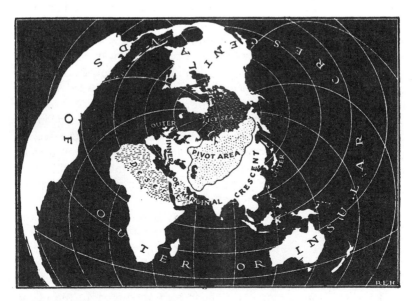

(b) The Mackinder map transferred to an azimuthal equidistant projection centring on the Pivot area.

Source: Weigert, H.W. and Stefansson, V. (eds.), *Compass of the World* (Harrap & Co. Ltd., London, 1944).

very important in intercontinental communications. This is something which Stefansson, who saw a great future for the Arctic, had been stressing for some time. He envisaged this 'Northern Mediterranean' as the hub of the air communications of the future as the great circle air routes connecting the major centres of population crossed over it. He also saw its future in the context of 'the northward march of empire' and the historic northward movement of the centres of civilisation. The Arctic climate, he contended, was more hospitable than was generally believed and far less hazardous for aircraft than were the sub-arctic regions. He also believed that there were considerable natural resources there awaiting exploitation. When the great potential value of the area came to be more fully appreciated, he said, 'then will the basin of the Arctic Mediterranean at last come into its own, judged by its real merits and demerits, no longer by folk beliefs which we have inherited from our intellectual ancestors, the subtropical Egyptians, Hebrews, Greeks and Romans who dwelt around the Old World's lesser Mediterranean'.[13]

This also entailed, according to Burden, a reorientation of America's relationship with the rest of the world. Since the foundation of the republic, the United States had always looked on Europe as being the world's commercial, cultural and diplomatic centre. In the context of new world realities it was now time for this to be changed: 'Our schools and colleges must rise to the challenge, so that future Americans may face northward with the same resolute confidence with which their ancestors faced the West.'[14] The great powers of this new Arctic world would, in the nature of things, be the Soviet Union, Canada and the United States (Alaska). Stefansson, Weigert and Lattimore all felt it to be imperative that their own country should take up this new challenge without delay just as the Soviet Union was seen to be doing.

Not all American political geographers were as euphoric about the possibilities of the Arctic as a sort of new 'West', and some of them felt that to overemphasise them could lead to a distortion of reality as great as that perpetrated by Mercator. Both Burden and Spykman considered that the Arctic would long remain a hostile and difficult environment for those nurtured in more temperate latitudes. The reality was that the great centres of world power were in the mid-latitudes and were likely to remain so into the foreseeable future. Many of the great circle routes which connected them did not actually penetrate the Arctic regions. Burden envisaged the air routes of the future as being in any case relatively short-haul affairs due to the necessity for refuelling and picking up passengers in the manner of the train or bus.

The principal thrust of this new 'azimuthal' view of America's position in the world was, of necessity, towards the north. It was therefore removed both in direction and in policy from the older hemispheric concerns which had been of such importance since the enunciation of the Monroe Doctrine in the early nineteenth century (see page 85, Note 47). This had, in fact, fitted in with isolationist attitudes since isolation from the Old World had in no way precluded the development of a constructive relationship with the New. This was the basis of Roosevelt's 'good neighbour' policy which was contrasted to advantage with the 'bad neighbour' policy of the Nazis in Europe. The hegemonial power of the Americas was seen to conduct its international affairs in a very different manner from those seeking hegemony over Eurasia. Americans of most political persuasions recognised and accepted that their country had a special role to play in this area. It was in this direction too that the German *Geopolitiker* themselves advocated that the United States should look rather than concern herself with the affairs of Europe.

The American political geographers recognised this role and particularly emphasised the importance to the United States of the Gulf of Mexico and the Caribbean. In this 'American Mediterranean', as Weigert referred to it, the United States was the dominant littoral country with vital interests in procuring raw materials, providing for hemispheric defence and securing the Panama Canal. Its opening in 1914 had had the effect, as Spykman put it, of turning the country around on its axis, and making her for the first time a truly Pacific as well as Atlantic power.

Over and above the relationship of the United States to the lands to the south and to the north, there loomed, in the early 1940s, the question of her relationship with Eurasia. The geopolitical starting point in coming to terms with this was the thesis of the dichotomy of land power and sea power inherited from the European geographers. Taylor re-emphasised the concept of the British Empire as a great swathe of sea power around the continent and the Soviet Union as the dominant land power. From 1941 both were in alliance and he envisaged that pressure exerted in unison from both land and sea could crush the enemy powers as between the upper and the nether millstones.[15] Lattimore, viewing the world through the eyes of the landsman, saw the crumbling of the four-hundred-year-old maritime predominance of the Europeans, and with it the imminent end of British world power. The emerging successor states were those of the Asian continent, in particular the Soviet Union and China:

> The age in which Asia was penetrated and developed from its fringes toward the center is drawing to an end. A new age is opening out in which the focus for development will lie at or near the center and the effect of this development will radiate outward to the fringes.[16]

He felt that the Europeans were unlikely to accept this development readily, but would try their best to prolong their influence. After their defeat, he foresaw the possibility of Japan and Germany being maintained as bastions in the maintenance of maritime power but he felt that this would be both a pointless and an unwise policy.

Spykman saw three great centres of world power, these consisting of 'the Atlantic coastal regions of North America, the European littoral and the Far Eastern coastland of Eurasia'.[17] A possible fourth was India which, although at the time insignificant, had the capacity to develop in the future. Of the three Eurasian regions, the European littoral was the one of greatest importance to the United States. This was both because America originated as a transatlantic projection of European civilisation and also because the most important regions in the United States were naturally oriented eastwards towards the Atlantic.

Despite the fact that such a divergence of views was expressed by the advocates of an American global strategy, the more influential of America's political geographers were of the opinion that their country had no option after 1940 but to align herself with Britain. For Spykman the victory of the German-Japanese alliance would have meant their achieving joint control over the three great power centres in Eurasia. America would then have been reduced to a position of considerable vulnerability since, although powerful, she could not have resisted a combination of all the other major powers. In order to survive as a world power she had thus no choice but to go to the assistance of Britain. Nations which renounce the power struggle, as he put it, and 'deliberately choose impotence ... risk eventual absorption by powerful neighbours'.[18]

On this matter Weigert was of a similar opinion and he felt that Britain and America had had great good fortune — far more than they deserved — in having the Soviet Union and China as their allies. Without the great capacity for survival displayed by these two powers against incredible odds, it was probable that British resistance would have crumbled and America would be facing alone a united and hostile Eurasia.

In 1944 Spykman analysed the geopolitical features of the European and Far Eastern war fronts.[19] By that time it had become clear that both the German and the Japanese attempts to achieve regional hegemonies had failed, despite the great advantages they enjoyed of having been able to concentrate their strength into relatively compact triangles (Figure 7.2). It was the combination of the land power of Russia and China and the sea power of Britain and America which he saw as having forced them both to wage war simultaneously on their maritime and their continental fronts. The failure of either the Germans or the Japanese to dispose of any one front and so be able to concentrate all their strength on the other represented the real turning point of the struggle. Despite serious initial reverses the continental and maritime powers had been able to retreat to safety and carry on the struggle out of range of the enemy. It was still vital in 1943 for the United States to continue to develop its enormous potential so as to give aid to its allies on both fronts. The problems in providing this assistance to the Eurasian allies had been exacerbated by German submarine strength in the Atlantic and by Japanese control of South-East Asia, so cutting off China from India. It was this situation which revealed the great potential importance of the Arctic routes as the safest and most direct lines of communication amongst the allies. However, in practice the adverse weather conditions and the great distances involved were obstacles too great for the technology of the time, and they remained of peripheral importance.

Behind the actual strategy of America's involvement in the war there was the discussion of the nature of the world which was to be created when it was over. It was here that there appeared the most serious differences of view among American political geographers, and, while each of them had his own unique viewpoint, there was an overall divergence into two distinct schools of thought. These may be termed the idealists and the realists and on occasion considerable acrimony was engendered in the course of their debates.

Figure 7.2: Territories Occupied by Germany and Japan in 1942

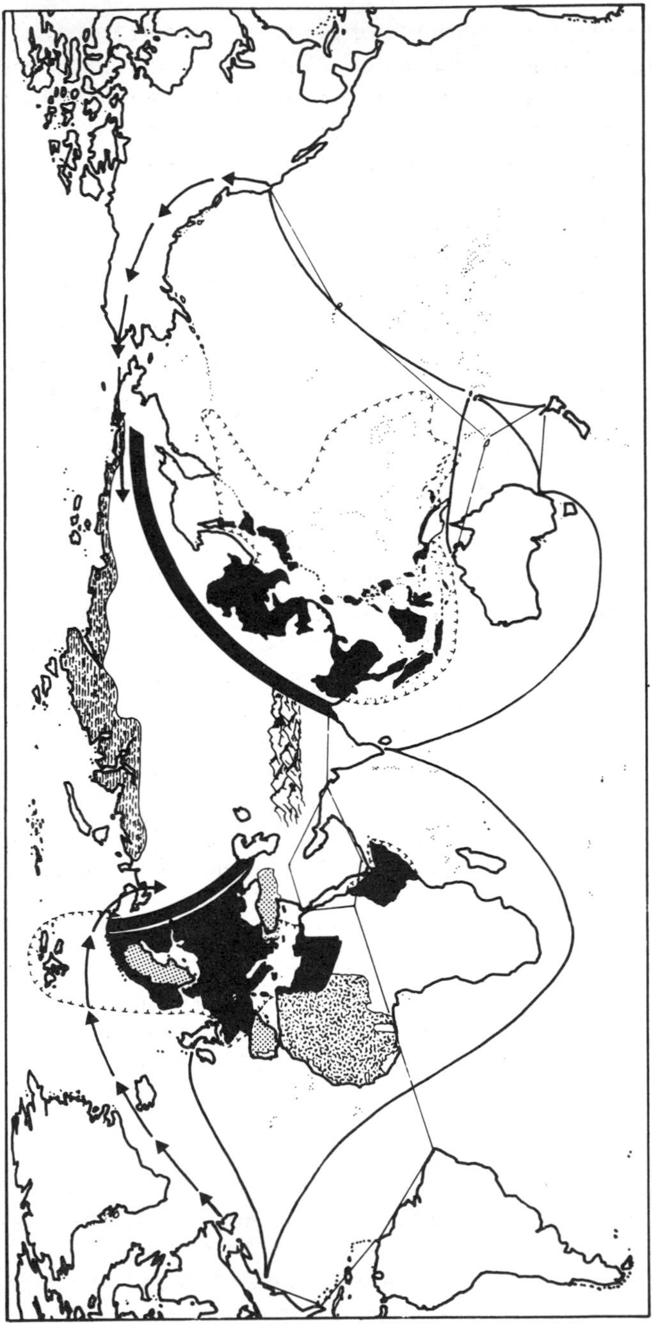

Source: *The Geography of the Peace*, N.J. Spykman, (Harcourt, Brace and Co., New York, 1944).

The idealist viewpoint arose from the older traditions of American political geography, particularly identified with the names of Bowman, Hartshorne and Whittlesey. They believed that, given the nature of the subject matter, political geography should always be studied as academically as possible. It should normally eschew the attempt to discover 'laws', since generalisation of that sort could be dangerous particularly when founded, as so often happened, upon insufficient evidence. They considered a rigorous and objective analysis of the world as it is to be the most effective counter to geopolitically-induced chauvinism.[20] Above all, the study should be dedicated to the understanding of real men, as Weigert put it, rather than to easy generalisations about mankind as a whole. Their ideals were founded on the Wilsonian tradition of international morality as enunciated in the Fourteen Points and the Covenant of the League of Nations. They were convinced that America's international stance should be governed by the highest considerations, and that their country should be a model to others in the principles and practice of good neighbourliness in the world. They wished to extend the ideals and values on which the Republic had been founded to the organisation of the world as a whole. Power politics was roundly condemned as having brought the world to its present sorry pass, and it was something with which America should in no circumstances be involved.

The idealist viewpoint was most radically voiced by Edmund Walsh who condemned *Geopolitik* as the logical culmination of that process of secularisation which had been taking place since the Renaissance and the Industrial Revolution.[21] This emphasised the 'autonomy and primacy of the material' and was now expressed in the deification of the state. It was Walsh's opinion that a better world would never be created until the spirit of man had been purged of gross materialism. An American geopolitics had to be founded on higher ideals than that. 'Geopolitics can ennoble as well as corrupt. It can choose between two alternatives — the value of power or the power of values.' He proposed a recall to office of Mackinder's airy cherub whose warnings had gone unheeded by the statesmen gathered at Versailles a quarter of a century before. The first piece of advice to the new peacemakers should be: 'Do not imagine that the Anglo-American program for a reconstructed world has descended direct from Sinai.'

In a more down-to-earth vein, Derwent Whittlesey emphasised the importance of a sound knowledge of the realities of the world in order to be able to construct a lasting peace. In order to establish 'a world imbued with a mutual will to peaceful neigh-bourliness', he contended, it was essential to have 'an understand-ing of the earth-base of human society at least equal to that possessed by the better informed Germans'.[22] The new world order should be based upon an improved relationship between the generally passive peoples of the tropics and the aggressive peoples of the middle latitudes, and also between the Occident and the Orient. He proposed the solution of problems in the context of a world organisation. Since the Middle Ages, larger political units had been evolving and the next logical step was towards some kind of global federation. The alternative to this, he warned, would be the emergence of new great powers which would move towards competition and eventually to war. The only lasting answer to the world's problems was thus through co-operation.

Lattimore was particularly concerned that the new world order should provide freedom and justice for the oppressed peoples of the world.[23] Dismissing the Japanese battle cry of 'Asia for the Asiatics' as merely a cover for an even harsher form of imperialism, he was of the opinion that America's stance at that time was an inadequate one. He focused attention on what he regarded as being the central flaw of the 'integrated imperialism and democracy' which America was then bolstering. 'The world can no longer survive half democratic and half colonial, half sub-ject and half free.' European imperialism had to be brought to an end, and such great countries as the Soviet Union, China and India had to be fully independent and respected. The old world order had to be encouraged to give place to the new: 'Our problem is not how to control this development, but how to adapt ourselves to it.'

Among the most realistic of the idealists was Weigert, who admonished that moralistic chiding from the sidelines was far from being an adequate response on its own: 'We should not attack the creed of geopolitics hypocritically standing on lofty heights, and look down with horror at the bloody ground on which the *Geo-politiker* assemble their forces.'[24] Like the others he was of the opinion that the Americans had to learn from German *Geopolitik*, but had also to learn to use it constructively. He agreed with Lattimore in the latter's criticism of American connivance at Euro-pean colonialism. It should be America's task in the post-war world both to assist in the full liberation of Eurasia and to encourage the development of freedom and democracy there. The real bond between the peoples of North America and Eurasia should be in their combined opposition to all forms of imperialism and their determination to work with and not against the new realities in the world. 'Ours is not the task of re-establishing over-thrown sovereignties,' he said, and he envisaged an idealistic role for his 'humanised geopolitics'.

Such were some of the variety of views expressed by those advocating the central position of ideals in the new geopolitics. The views of those advocating *Realpolitik* were also diverse. They ranged from those of Renner and Beukema who largely accepted German *Geopolitik* to Staley who criticised the 'Maginot men-tality' of the 'Western Hemisphere complex' and advocated instead 'a world-girdling defence area based on joint British and American sea power'. However, the unifying belief of the realist school of thought was that America should abandon the psychology of apartness and enter the lists as a full protagonist in the global power game. It was only by so doing, they felt, that America could be strong and secure. Spykman was the most influential of these realists, and he stated his position quite categorically:

> Neither the self-evident truth of our principles nor the divine basis of our moral values is in itself enough to assure a world built in the image of our aspirations ... Force is manifestly an indispensable instrument both for national survival and for the creation of a better world.[25]

The world organisation, so cherished by the idealists, he con-sidered from the outset as unrealistic, since it did not take into account the realities of the world in which we live. These realities he saw as being that different states had different sets of values which they sought to promote; that states were at many different stages of economic and political development and were therefore unlikely to find one organisation acceptable to them all; and that some were satisfied and some dissatisfied with the existing inter-national status quo, the latter being inclined to rectify the situation by the use of force. On these grounds he totally rejected the premise that there was a world community which was ready and waiting to support the formation of an effective international organisation.

Spykman's vision of the post-war world was firmly based upon his perception of the realities of the distribution of power in the world. Since he considered that the central danger to America during World War II arose from the possibility of the union of the Eurasian power centres against the United States, he believed that it was essential in the future that such a situation should never be allowed to recur. He foresaw a future power struggle taking place between France, Germany and Eastern Europe for the dominant position in Europe, with Germany, because of her natural advantages, being the most likely victor. In the Far East he foresaw the emergence of China as the hegemonial power. It was not in the interests of the British or the Americans that either eventuality should be allowed to take place. In order to counter it, support should be given to France in Europe and to Japan in the Far East. Such support could be most effective if given by the 'Big Three' acting in unison to ensure that an adequate distribution of power was preserved. Pressure outwards by the Soviet Union itself, particularly towards China, was another likely factor in the post-war world.

Thus Spykman did not advocate the destruction of the power of the enemy countries, but their retention on the international scene as necessary counterweights in the world balance of power. His advocacy of the continuation into peacetime of the alliance of the United States, Britain and the Soviet Union arose from his belief that there was no other way in which they would be able to maintain their security. Not one of them had sufficient power to be able to achieve this alone, and he saw the situation of the Soviet Union as being a particularly vulnerable one. It was thus common sense for the United States to maintain an alliance with her, and to project power northwards into the Arctic in order to develop and maintain secure lines of communication. Although far from being as euphoric about the Arctic as were Weigert and Stefansson, he still believed in its crucial strategic importance. It would be America's 'third front' after the Atlantic and Pacific, and in the coming air age it would quickly dwarf the other two since it was closer to the major centres of power in Eurasia. In this way what he referred to as 'the three super-powers' were together to be the guarantors of world peace and they could do this most effectively if an equilibrium of power were maintained among them. In this context it is interesting that he appeared to foresee more possibility of altercation between America and Britain over maritime zones of influence than between America and the Soviet Union. The latter he felt to be 'the most effective continental base for the enforcement of peace'. The Soviet Union was thus to take over the position held until then by France, now seen as too weak and ineffective, in relation to British and American maritime power. The answer to the problem of world peace for Spykman therefore lay not with the Utopian dreams of a world federation nor yet with British and American maritime dominance, which would only stimulate a countervailing continental alliance. Rather it lay in a balance among the major centres of world power in the post-European age.

Spykman's new *Realpolitik* came in for considerable criticism from the idealists. Weigert, who was of the opinion that each nation got the geopolitics it deserved, felt that this was little better than that of the Germans themselves. This was certainly not the diet of vitamins, but a remedy which was almost as bad as the disease. To him Spykman's ideas were a 'corrupting *Weltanschauung* ... that does not differ at all from the philosophy of Haushofer's Prussian militarism'.[26] Blinded as they were, he said, by the overwhelming might of a world-wide scheme of power politics, the advocates of *Realpolitik* ignored such ephemerals as justice, freedom, ethics and the Sermon on the Mount. Rather they conducted a cold chess game of power politics, using as their motto, as did Haushofer — *si vis pacem para bellum.*[27] To this philosophy he opposed Vice-President Wallace's 'Those who write the peace must think of the whole world'. One of Gyorgy's principal criticisms of Spykman was that, despite his strenuous denials, he was actually very determinist in his attitudes.[28] He saw the alliance which Spykman proposed as being a sort of regionalised League of Nations and did not consider either this or the balance of power as at all adequate as safeguards of world peace.

Thus the debate within American political geography in the early 1940s centred on a number of quite fundamental issues. It was between the co-operators and the confronters; between those who felt that the peace could most effectively be secured through working together with other nations and those who felt that the surest way to achieve national security lay through strength. The latter, in general, subscribed to some form of determinism, believing that the broad course was charted and would have to be followed if disaster were not to ensue, while the former believed that 'natural' geopolitical processes could, and should, be transcended. It was accepted that, in the past, the struggle for power had been the world's international leitmotiv. However, it was maintained that this did not have to go on being so, that it could be different, and that the United States was the country above all others which could make it so. Fundamentally this great debate was between those who believed in the ultimate goodness of humanity and those who were constrained to be prudent in the face of much historical evidence to the contrary.

There were, however, a number of points of agreement. It was generally agreed that America's emergence onto the centre of the world stage was now permanent. There could be no return to the isolation of the inter-war years. There was also broad agreement that *Geopolitik* had to be understood and an American form of geopolitics forged to counter it. There was agreement that American ideals and values were to be cherished and that the object of any course of action was to protect the American way of life.

The American political geographers of the period around World War II were thus by no means ivory-tower academics. They were involved in a good deal of proselytising on behalf of their new ideas and the national enthusiasm for 'barbershop geopolitics' was triggered off by many articles on the subject in newspapers and magazines. With the outbreak of war this became for a time almost a sort of missionary endeavour aiming to convert the American people and their leaders to the importance of the geographical viewpoint in the understanding of world affairs. Its principal thrust was against the evils of German *Geopolitik* and a complete refutation of all that it stood for. The new political geography was thus, in the broadest sense, a part of the war effort and took an unequivocally American standpoint. In this it was doing no more than following Bowman, the grand old man of American political geography. Whilst always championing the value of the dispassionate study of the world scene, the four editions of *The New World*[29] were nevertheless imbued with a thoroughly American sense of righteousness. Described as being a 'Wilsonian Democrat' he had been an important member of the President's team at Versailles and had acted as co-ordinator of all geographical matters. He subsequently remained in a position to influence policy and during World War II worked as Geographer at the State Department, in this capacity attending many important international gatherings. By then he had formed the opinion that the importance of geographical thinking had come to be widely accepted. 'At first we thought of security in terms of the mollusc, the hemisphere was our shield,' he wrote in 1942.[30] Then, following Nazi aggression in Europe, there came a realisation that there had to be resistance and 'all of us began to think geographically and to regard the map in terms of political ideas and systems'. As a result, he maintained, there was no possibility of a return to the comforting 'limited liability' attitudes of the past.

Franklin Delano Roosevelt, who had been President since 1933, was himself an amateur geographer and had been a member of the Council of the American Geographical Society. He had always taken a particular interest in naval matters and at an early age had absorbed the naval doctrines of Admiral Mahan, who had sown seeds in many minds, including that of Franklin's uncle, President Theodore Roosevelt. Franklin owned to being an 'eager pupil and apprentice' of Mahan and was convinced of the importance of a knowledge of geography to the understanding of world affairs.[31] He knew Bowman well, and during the war consulted with him on a number of occasions. He was, in common with his fellow countrymen, himself evolving a world view, and initially this owed much to Mahan and Mackinder. It was coloured by his belief in Wilsonian liberalism and out of it came the conviction that America would be forced to take part in the coming war whether she liked the idea or not. In the late 1930s he made strenuous efforts to combat the latent isolationism in America and to prepare his nation psychologically for the coming struggle. This gained a new urgency with the outbreak of war in Europe in September 1939 and especially after the collapse of France in June 1940. Britain was now alone, an outpost of the maritime world perched precariously on the edge of German-dominated Europe. His conviction was that, in her own interest, America had now to follow a 'good-neighbour policy' in regard to Britain, and he therefore urged his country to become 'the arsenal for democracy'. Ingenious devices, such as the Lend-Lease arrangement, were found to send aid to the beleaguered British for the 18 months from the fall of France until America entered the war. The historic meeting of Roosevelt and Churchill at Placentia Bay, New-foundland, in August 1941 produced the Atlantic Charter and served to draw the two maritime powers still closer together. The subsequent Anglo-American naval co-operation was seen by the historian J.P. Lash as being 'a further expression of the prophetic doctrine' of Mahan, and a move towards what Henry Adams had called 'the Atlantic System'.[32] With American entry into the war in

December 1941 following the Japanese attack on Pearl Harbor, the 'North Atlantic Triangle' of Britain, the United States and Canada became the geopolitical focus of the resistance of the maritime world to the three aggressor states.

From then on, Roosevelt was also firmly in pursuit of good relations with the Soviet Union. The leaders of the principal allies, now dubbed the 'Big Three', met at Teheran in 1943 and again at Yalta in 1945, and these meetings led him to the conviction that friendship with the Soviets should be possible. In this he was far more euphoric than Churchill, or for that matter many of his own fellow countrymen. The latter, particularly those not of the President's political persuasion, were already coming round to the view that their Russian ally could in time become as big a menace as was their current enemy. However, despite the difficulties, the cultivation of good Russo-American relations became central to Roosevelt's thinking right up to his untimely death in April 1945. He had in this respect moved away from vintage Mahan and Mackinder and towards the views of Spykman and those who were of a similar geopolitical persuasion.

Within five years of the end of World War II America had been engulfed by the harsh international climate of the Cold War. Wilsonian, and now Rooseveltian, liberalism rapidly gave place to harder attitudes. America, like the rest of the world, entered a power struggle between 'East' and 'West' without even the brief idealistic breathing space which had followed World War I. America's response was indeed a new Monroe Doctrine, initially in the form of the Truman Declaration of 1947, which legitimised American intervention in the affairs of Eurasia. It was certainly a world corresponding more closely to the vision of Spykman than those of either Weigert or Walsh, although the actual course followed by the new *Realpolitik* was very different from that advocated and predicted by the great realist himself.

Notes

1. C. Ross, 'Amerika greift nach der Weltmacht', *Zeitschrift fur Geopolitik*, 16 (1939).

2. I. Bowman, 'Geography versus Geopolitics', *Geographical Review*, XXXII, 4 (1942).

3. H.W. Weigert, *Generals and Geographers: The Twilight of Geopolitics* (Oxford University Press, New York, 1942).

4. N.J. Spykman, *America's Strategy in World Politics* (Harcourt Brace, New York, 1942).

5. H.W. Weigert, *Generals and Geographers: The Twilight of Geopolitics*, Chapter 1.

6. Ibid.

7. R. Strausz-Hupé, *Geopolitics: The Struggle for Space and Power* (Putman, New York, 1942).

8. D. Whittlesey, *German Strategy of World Conquest* (Robinson, London, 1942).

9. A. Gyorgy, *Geopolitics — The New German Science* (University of California Press, Berkeley, 1944).

10. A. Dorpalen, *The World of General Haushofer* (Farrar and Rinehart, New York, 1942).

11. R.E. Harrison, and H.W. Weigert, 'World View and Strategy' in H.W. Weigert and V. Stefansson (eds.), *Compass of the World: A Symposium on Political Geography* (Harrap, London, 1943).

12. V. Stefansson, 'The Logic of the Air', *Fortune*, 4 (1943).

13. Ibid.

14. W.A.M. Burden, 'American Air Transport Faces North' in H.W. Weigert and V. Stefansson, *Compass of the World*.

15. G. Taylor, 'Canada's Role in Geopolitics' in H.W. Weigert and V. Stefansson, *Compass of the World*.

16. O. Lattimore, 'The Inland Crossroads of Asia' in H.W. Weigert and V. Stefansson, *Compass of the World*.

17. N.J. Spykman, *America's Strategy in World Politics*.

18. Ibid.

19. N.J. Spykman, *The Geography of the Peace* (Harcourt Brace, New York, 1944).

20. I. Bowman, *The New World*, 4th edn, (Harrap, London, 1928)

21. E.A. Walsh, 'Geopolitics and International Morals' in H.W. Weigert and V. Stefansson, *Compass of the World*.

22. D. Whittlesey, *German Strategy of World Conquest*.

23. O. Lattimore, 'The Inland Crossroads of Asia'.

24. H.W. Weigert, *Generals and Geographers: The Twilight of Geopolitics*.

25. N.J. Spykman, *The Geography of the Peace*.

26. R.E. Harrison and H.W. Weigert, 'World View and Strategy'.

27. He who would have peace must prepare for war.

28. A. Gyorgy, *Geopolitics — the New German Science*.

29. I. Bowman, *The New World*, 4 editions, (Harrap, London and World Book, New York, 1922, 1924, 1926 and 1928).

30. I. Bowman, 'Geography versus Geopolitics'.

31. J.P. Lash, *Roosevelt and Churchill 1939–41: The Partnership that Saved the West* (Norton, New York, 1976).

32. Ibid.

8 HEARTLAND REVISITED: NEW PERSPECTIVES AFTER WORLD WAR II

In 1954 Hartshorne asserted that the Pivot had become the most famous contribution of modern geography to man's view of his political world.[1] He prefixed this statement with the words 'for better or worse', and indeed subsequent discussion of the whole Pivot-Heartland subject has taken place in largely partisan terms.

Its principal opponents have been dismissive, but by implication they accept its importance by returning to do battle yet again. One detects an uneasy feeling, rather like that of some agnostics about religion, that there could, after all, be something in it. The ghost never seemed to be completely laid according to Blacksell, and Muir complained that despite frequent refutation it rose again 'phoenix-like for further punishment'.[2]

The criticisms levelled against it have been manifold. To Malin it was racialist and Eurocentric, and quite indefensible in both terminology and ideas. Sprout felt that it greatly overemphasised the importance of location as opposed to other factors contributing to national strength. Jones questioned the elements of determinism which it contained, particularly when it had been twisted into the fatalistic doctrine of '*Herzland über alles*'.[3] Short saw the theory as having provided the strategic rationale for the British presence overseas and as having sanctified imperialism and legitimised it into the need to protect democracy.[4] To others, such as Blouet, it was essentially a product of its time.[5]

Parker countered by claiming that the critics themselves had often failed to understand the full meaning of the ideas they were so ready to criticise.[6] He maintained that Mackinder's profound knowledge of both history and geography made him well aware of the difficulties inherent in his broad canvas. This was inevitably one of the problems faced by those who aimed to make bold interpretations. As Mackinder himself had put it in 1890: 'No science can satisfy the mind which does not allow the building of palaces out of the bricks.'[7] Gilbert and Parker in their assessment of the whole matter in 'Mackinder's *Democratic Ideals and Reality* after Fifty Years', stood convinced of the continuing validity of the theory in the 1960s.[8] In 1919, they said, it had been too far ahead of its time to make an impact, but its relevance had increased with the passing of the years. They saw it as being deep down a much needed reminder to men so that 'however high they may lift their heads among the clouds [they] may be ever mindful of the need to keep their feet firmly planted on the earth's surface'. Parker also rejected the charge of determinism which had been levelled from many quarters. Mackinder, he said, was giving warning of what could happen if the course of events went unchecked, rather than positively attempting to foretell the future. It was for man himself, through the exercise of his free will, to take control of his destiny and in this way to prevent the occurrence of the worst of the possible eventualities.

Of more significance in the development of geopolitical thought were those modifications made to the theory during and after World War II. A number of these emerged in the context of developments in American political geography outlined in Chapter 7. However, one of the first to return to the Heartland was none other than Mackinder himself who in 1943, at the age of 82, produced his third and final major statement. In his article 'The Round World and the Winning of the Peace'[9] he judged that his thesis was now more useful than ever. 'The Heartland is the greatest natural fortress on earth. For the first time in history it is manned by a garrison sufficient in both number and quality.' However, he radically modified its area, this time to exclude 'Lenaland', his name for the huge territories to the east of the Yenisei river. If the Soviet Union defeated Germany, he said, then she would emerge from the war as the strongest land power on the globe. The principal objects of the post-war settlement would be to curtail German aggression and to sweep clear 'the polluted channel' of Nazi ideology. These objectives could only be satisfactorily achieved through the alliance of land and sea power, the latter centred on 'the three amphibious powers' of America, Great Britain and France. Each had its particular role, 'the first for depth of defence, the second as a moated forward stronghold — a Malta on a grander scale — and the third as a defensible bridgehead'. The combination of the land power to the east in the Heartland and the sea power to the west in the basin of the North Atlantic, would then constitute two unshakeable fronts, one on either side, so that 'the Devil in Germany ... must die of inanition'.

Mackinder then turned his eye to the world scene and perceived it in a very different light from that of a quarter of a century earlier. A central feature of the canvas was now that huge belt of mountains, wastes and deserts encircling the earth in the Northern Hemisphere. It included the Sahara, the deserts of Central Asia and the Arctic and sub-Arctic wastelands of Siberia and North America. This formed 'a girdle hung around the north-polar regions' and enclosed within it were the redefined Heartland together with the 'Midland Ocean' (North Atlantic). This vast area stretching from the Missouri to the Yenisei had a combined population of 1,000 million, and it formed a 'twin unit' of balanced power. This he saw as being geopolitically the fulcrum of the earth and he called it his 'second geographical concept'. A great 'mantle of vacancies', part of the Northern Hemisphere 'girdle', separated this from the other major populous region of the world, the monsoon lands of India and China. As it grew in strength, this area could eventually become a counterweight to the Northern Hemisphere. This vision led Mackinder to end on a note of unclouded optimism when he foresaw 'a balanced globe of human beings. And happy because balanced and thus free'.

The 1943 article was a fundamental departure from earlier ideas. The 'second geographical concept' with its linkage of the revised Heartland and the Midland Ocean was now the 'fulcrum' and so effectively took over from the Heartland. It resulted from the alliance of land and sea power in the Northern Hemisphere, and was thus in contradiction to the dichotomy of land and sea power fundamental to the interpretations of 1904 and 1919. It implicitly acknowledged the fact that in both world wars continental and maritime power had been in alliance, and it extrapolated from this the conviction that such an alliance had to continue if peace were to be preserved. In common with others at the time, he was also now looking at 'the round world' and what he perceived was very different from the Mercator projection of the previous analyses. The Heartland was considerably reduced both in size and in significance and the Midland Ocean appeared as the major focus of the activities of mankind. The major world balance was no longer between land and sea power, but between the northern fulcrum and the Monsoon lands. These two greatest centres of mankind were conveniently separated from each other by a huge negative zone and presumably as a direct result of this, they were not regarded as being potentially in conflict with each other.

Walters considered that in effect Mackinder abandoned his

Figure 8.1: Variations on the Heartland Theme

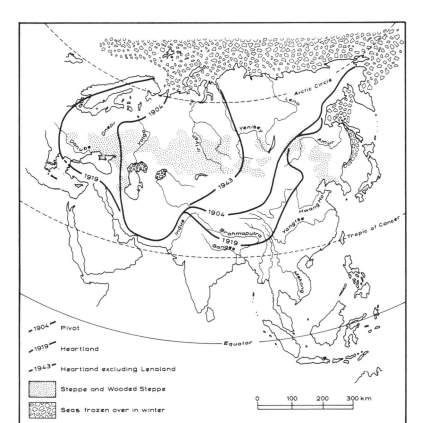

Heartland theory altogether in 1943.[10] Certainly it is clear that a different thesis of global power relationships was now conjured up by the old master. In his twilight years he hoped for a continuation into peacetime of the Grand Alliance which was by 1943 turning the tide against the enemy powers both in Europe and in the Far East. In this he was at one with the idealistic school of American political geographers. Perhaps it was wishful thinking which led him to devise the scenario which was most likely, in his view, to maintain world peace in the future.

In the year following Mackinder's new 'round world' vision, Spykman returned to the original Heartland theory.[11] In doing so, he challenged its validity and expressed considerable doubt as to the region's capacity to sustain the role of world conqueror. He found it to be wanting in almost every respect, questioning even its strategic advantages in the modern world. He gave his attention rather to the Inner Crescent (see Chapter 3) which he saw as possessing far more tangible attributes of world power. It was well endowed in population, resources and wealth and around it was 'a circumferential maritime highway which links the whole area together in terms of sea power'. Beyond it lay the off-shore islands of Britain, Africa, the East Indies, Australasia and Japan. Spykman substantially extended the area covered by the Inner Crescent to include virtually all continental Europe west of the Baltic-Black Sea isthmus, the mountainous centre of Asia and the whole of China, and he christened it the 'Rimland' (Figure 8.2). In world power terms he saw it functioning as a 'vast buffer zone of conflict between sea power and land power. Looking in both directions it must function amphibiously and defend itself on land and sea'.

This leads on to the nub of Spykman's argument, which was that Mackinder's assertion that land and sea power are in conflict is historically false. The Mackinder theory was, in fact, based upon a constellation of forces which existed only at a particular time. While it operated through most of the nineteenth century, it had come to an end with the Anglo-Russian *entente* of 1907. The reality had actually been a much more complicated one than this. According to Spykman, it had consisted either of situations in which land power and sea power had been allied against an intervening Rimland state or ones in which some Rimland states allied to continental power were in opposition to other Rimland states allied to maritime power. From this he deduced that the Mackinder dictum must be false and that it should therefore be replaced by: 'Who rules the Rimland rules Eurasia; who rules Eurasia controls the destinies of the world.'

Spykman was of the opinion that the Rimland would in future have far less unity than it had possessed when dominated by European, and in particular British, sea power. However, new centres of power were now emerging within it, and this would add to its potential strength in relation to continental power. As has been shown earlier, it was Spykman's belief that America's national interest lay in ensuring that the Rimland was never united under any single power. This, in his view, was the real object of America's participation in World War II. America's future course

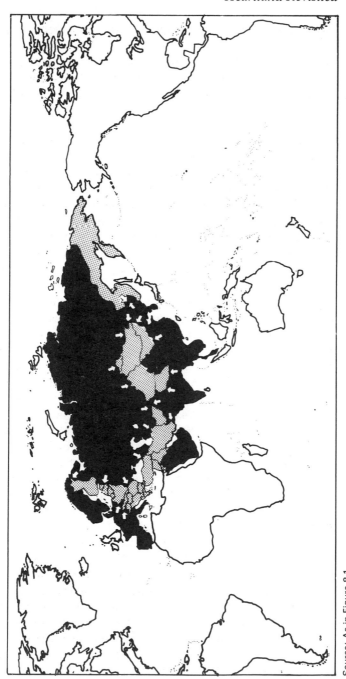

Figure 8.2: Heartland versus Rimland

Source: As in Figure 8.1.

of action should therefore be to ally herself with certain Rimland powers, and possibly also with the Heartland power itself. Spykman was aware of Mackinder's new departure, and he used it in order to add weight to his own arguments. He maintained that the advocacy of the continued alliance of the 'Big Three' after the war was an implicit recognition of the importance of the Rimland in world affairs.

Weigert, a firm opponent of many of Spykman's ideas, took a less indulgent view of the later Mackinder. In his *Heartland Revisited*, published in 1949, he dismissed the new balance as 'too neat and perfect to be true', and condemned it as being 'a structure built on shifting sand'.[12] He preferred to return to the original concept of the Heartland which he still saw as the greatest citadel of land power, now mightier than it had ever been before. This he explained by the rapid development of Central Asia and the Soviet Union's northward movement into Siberia. Here the concepts of the Heartland and the Arctic Mediterranean came together in his mind, and he saw North America, on the opposite side of the Arctic Ocean, as being the world's other major power centre. It was the northward course of both the Soviet Union and the United States which was producing the new politico-geographic relationship between the two of them. World power now centred on their two heartlands, lying 'in destiny-laden proximity across the Pole'.

Renner, while not entirely dismissing the Heartland, also took a polar view of its global relationships.[13] His conclusion was that the term 'Heartland' had now to be expanded to incorporate all the great continental interiors located around the Arctic Mediterranean. Air mobility over the polar regions had now placed them in an entirely new relationship to one another.

Jones developed on this line of thought and argued that in the nuclear age the Heartland had lost much of its significance: 'In an all-out nuclear war with cities blasted from the face of the earth and even the countryside polluted with radio-active fall-out, "Heartland", "Rimland", "land power" and "sea power" are words with little significance.'[14] It certainly remained a power base, but one of a number in the contemporary world. He therefore proposed the separation of the terms 'Heartland' and 'Pivot area', thus divorcing economic from strategic significance. It was conceivable to him that the new Pivot area was the Arctic region which was now so strategically located in relation to the great powers of the

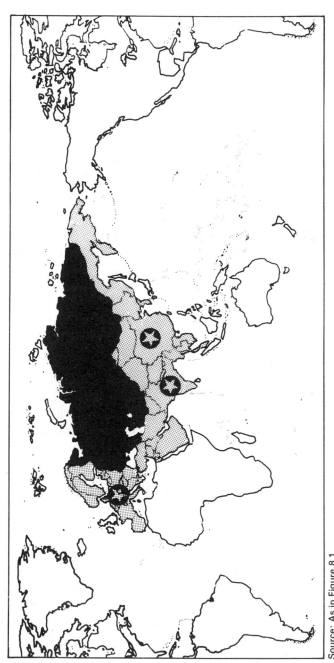

Figure 8.3: Conflict inside the Rimland

Source: As in Figure 8.1.

Northern Hemisphere. He envisaged this 'aerial Pivot area' having a role in the age of flight similar to that of Central Asia in the age of nomadic horsemen. However, he tempered this by casting doubts on the great future ascribed to the 'Northward Course' by its most ardent protagonists. He was of the opinion that 'there seems no reason to think that such booming cities as Murmansk, Igarka and Fairbanks will be the Moscows and New Yorks of the future'.

Cressey had even less time for the Heartland. Major weaknesses in the Mackinder thesis arose from insufficient attention to the roundness of the world and to the factors determining the value of geographical location.[15] He proposed nine geographical elements of power which included size, accessibility, location, minerals and climate, and examined the Heartland — 'this favourite field of writers in geopolitics' — in the light of these. In most of them he found it to be either positively lacking or not especially well endowed, and the environmental problems made it one of the most difficult areas to exploit. The level of physical resources was to him the most crucial determinant of the future locations of world power. During World War I the allies had 'floated to victory on a sea of oil. During World War II they flew to victory on a cloud of gasoline'. If there was a world Heartland, Cressey, writing in the late 1940s, felt that it must be in North America rather than in Asia. This continent was endowed with virtually all the geographical elements of power which Central Asia in large measure lacked, and it possessed the further advantage of 'a dynamic spirit'. He saw North America's future as bound up with the North Atlantic, this possibly becoming an Anglo-Saxon lake and the major centre of power in the world. In 1945 Cressey again examined the geographical elements of Russian strength and concluded, not surprisingly, that they were very limited.[16] He remained convinced that as a consequence of its very considerable physical disadvantages, a really significant world power was unlikely to be centred in the Heartland.

Fawcett's analysis of the post-war power situation was much more Mackinder-oriented than was that of Cressey.[17] To him the Heartland had become in some ways even more important, while in others it was now much less so. The Heartland was seen by Fawcett as being a region of lasting difficulty having little inherent potential for the generation of political power. However, its sheer size was bound to give considerable strategic advantage to its possessor. It was consequently externally based rather than indigenous power which had the potential for supremacy. The possibilities of achieving this depended upon the balance of land and sea power in the world at any one time. Diagonally across 'Mainland' (The World-Island) stretched an 'Inland Seaway' through the Mediterranean, the Red Sea and the Persian Gulf. Control over this was essential to the dominance exercised by sea power over the margins of Mainland. Since the balance of power was now moving in favour of the land, it seemed probable that this, together with other seas on the edge of the continent, could in future be denied to the maritime powers. If this occurred, then land-based power would be able to break through into Africa across the Middle Eastern land bridge. This would massively enlarge the effective area of the Heartland which could then become the strategic base for a greatly enhanced land power (Figure 8.4). Since the Heartland and its possible extension was separated from both India and China by a 'Great Divide' of mountain and desert, Fawcett agreed with Mackinder that its unification could most readily be achieved from Europe. A united Europe would possess sufficient power to make this happen, and so it followed that Europe had the potential for supremacy over 'Mainland' and then over the rest of the world.

While Fawcett envisaged the possibility of a greatly expanded Heartland, Meinig at the opposite extreme proposed a far smaller one.[18] In fact he restricted it to the very centre of Asia, land consisting for the most part of mountain and desert. Mackinder, he maintained, had been far too involved with the circumstances of his time for his concept to have much validity outside his period. For it to be made more relevant, it was necessary to base its delimitation on a set of functional criteria. The ones he chose were location, physical environment and culture, and by using these he delimited a Heartland which possessed a large measure of unity. Its principal significance lay in its centrality since it contained 'the nexus of all historic land routes interconnecting the several Rimland areas of China, India, the Levant and Europe'. He maintained that this had a greater historical-spatial validity than had the earlier version.

Meinig then went on to examine the features of the Rimland and, while basically accepting Spykman's definition, divided it into two parts, continental and maritime. The former looked inwards to the continent while the latter looked outwards to the ocean. This

Figure 8.4: The Heartland Extended

Source: Weigert, H.W. *et al.* (eds.), *New Compass of the World* (Macmillan, New York, 1949).

division was regarded as being a functional rather than a fixed geographical one, and the orientations could and did change throughout history. China, India, the Middle East and parts of Europe had all gone through both continental and maritime phases, and so the actual divide between the two Rimlands had tended to oscillate as time passed. Meinig does not observe any set patterns in such changes, seeking their explanation in the particular circumstances of individual countries at different periods. Meinig's system was thus a less rigid one than those of either Mackinder or Spykman, his object being rather to create a broad explanatory framework for a more effective interpretation of the world scene. Pounds, examining Meinig's ideas in the light of world conditions in the 1960s, was of the opinion that the Iron Curtain could be seen as a more precise boundary than ever between the continental and maritime Rimlands.[19]

A more recent modification of the Heartland was that of Hooson, writing in the early 1960s.[20] His principal concern, like that of Cressey, was with the power of the Soviet Union, but he reached some rather more positive conclusions about it. He examined a set of factors which included physical resources, agricultural potential, population, urbanisation and industrial growth and, on the basis of these, he had little reason to doubt that the Soviet Union had now emerged as a formidable world power. Identifying the core of the state as being in the south of European Russia, he observed a tendency for this to extend latitudinally into Asia. This was the Volga-Baykal zone which he whimsically thought might be either a coffin-shaped or a crib-shaped axis. This zone possessed considerable natural resources, was rapidly urbanising and was followed by the trans-Siberian railway link. It had become a powerful magnet for Soviet economic development, and as a consequence of this the centre of gravity of the Soviet Union was seen as having moved eastwards. This had profound implications both for the Soviet Union itself and for Central Asia as a whole. He regarded this latter as being, in the context of communism, a much more formidable centre of power than ever in the past: 'Within this Communist world the Volga-Baykal zone has the marks of a real continental stronghold.'

The Heartland concept, in one form or another, had proved sufficiently flexible to survive into the new age of aeroplanes, nuclear weapons and intercontinental missiles. However, another parallel strand of geopolitical thought, particularly in America, maintained that with the arrival on the scene of the atomic bomb, from August 1945 in fact, a quantum leap had been made in the technology of warfare, and that previous geopolitical concepts had thus been rendered meaningless. It had therefore become imperative to construct a new geography for the new age. The most influential development along these lines was the 'air view' which gained credence during and after World War II. During this period there was a wide divergence of opinion ranging from those who felt, like Mackinder himself, that air power was but a new arm obeying the same strategic rules as the other two and operating alongside them, to those who viewed it as being altogether of a different order of power. The most influential exponent of this latter 'all out' view was de Seversky,[21] and its principal cartographic expression was the azimuthal equidistant projection centred on the North Pole. De Seversky was firmly convinced that the United States should now concentrate on the air rather than on land or sea power. Only by so doing would it be possible for her to achieve supremacy over the Soviet Union, since American resources were too limited to allow for the building up of massive strength in other ways.

De Seversky divided the world into two great circles of air power, focusing respectively on the industrial hearts of the United States and of the Soviet Union. That of the United States covered most of the Western Hemisphere, whilst that of the Soviet Union covered the greater part of the World-Island. The two possessed approximately equal power over North America and Northern Eurasia, and this was the 'area of decision' within which the two industrial hearts were in striking distance of one another by strategic bombers. The key to world supremacy thus lay within this area and the United States had a number of strategic advantages, in particular her scientific and technological lead and the British Isles (*sic*) which he called 'our only tenable overseas base'. Apart from this, the defence of the United States was to be conducted from the Western Hemisphere, and Latin America, located in the rear of the United States on the Pole-centred projection, was to constitute a reserve economic hinterland.

There were many, including Jones, who foresaw dangers in this proposed 'air isolationism' within its defensive perimeter. They felt it to be essential to defend parts of the Rimland if the whole Western Hemisphere were not to become increasingly vulnerable to attack. In any case, de Seversky's assumptions were founded on the ranges of aircraft in the years immediately following World War II, and they were considerably weakened by the immense advances in weaponry which took place in the 1950s and the 1960s.

The subjection of the Heartland to the most rigorous examination certainly revealed its shortcomings in fulfilling the world role allotted to it by its protagonists from Mackinder on. Most of the tinkering with its boundaries did not really make radical changes to such attributes as its strategic location, physical conditions, resources and population potential. Yet it has remained ghostlike in the geopolitical wings as if awaiting some final corroboration or rejection.

Perhaps the truth is that it is not so much its real attributes which account for its persistence as its role in the international scene as perceived from the West since World War II. From the late 1940s this had come to be dominated by the global confrontation of the two antagonistic superpowers, and the Heartland theory took on a new lease of life in this context. At a time when it was again coming under strong, and frequently disapproving, scrutiny by political geographers, it was seized upon as a method of giving a new explanatory dimension to the world scene.

The Soviet Union had increasingly come to be viewed in the West as being a dangerously aggressive state, and it appeared to draw its great power from the remote fastnesses of Central Asia. This vast continental hinterland thus came to be fraught with menace, expressed in 'suggestive maps' portraying a gigantic and expanding red stain over Eurasia, so creating a geography of fear. During the 1950s, when the cold war was at its height, the Soviet Union and China, the two great communist superpowers, appeared welded together to form a gigantic bloc covering a third of the world's area and containing a similar proportion of its population. The Heartland in this context was the nexus of a concatenation of power greater than the West had faced since the hordes of Genghis Khan had streamed out of Asia in the thirteenth century. This massive bloc corresponded in area to the enlarged Heartland of 1919 with the addition of the whole of the Pacific coast of Asia from Kamchatka to the South China Sea. Mackinder himself, with considerable prescience and no small sense of foreboding, had speculated on such a possibility in 1904 when he had pointed to the danger of a Heartland organised by the Chinese rather than the Russians. He felt that such a development 'might constitute the yellow peril to the world's freedom just because they would add an oceanic frontage to the resources of the great continent, an advantage as yet denied to the Russian tenant of the Pivot region'. Sixty years later Hooson was of the opinion that the belief of Westerners in 'a geographically charmed sanctuary in the Eurasian interior ... has been immeasurably buttressed by [its] becoming the seat of World Communism, which now holds sway from the Elbe to the South China Sea'.[22] Indeed, with the close ideologically-based alliance between the two Asiatic giants, the Heartland as a geopolitical concept may have appeared barely ade-

Figure 8.5: The Heartland and the Cold War

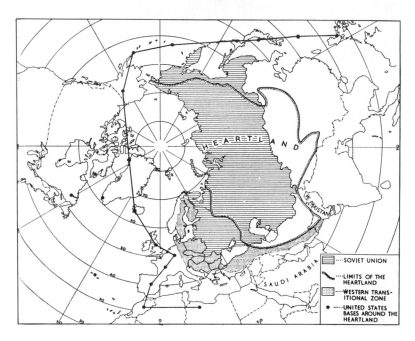

Source: East, W.G. and Moodie, A.C., *The Changing World* (Harrap and Co., London, 1956).

quate to describe the massive power now ranged against the West.

A linked aspect of Mackinder's theory which also made it appropriate to the post-war world situation was its fundamentally confrontational approach. This made it well adapted to the new age of global confrontation. Viewed from a longer perspective, the cold war could even be regarded as being a kind of reactivation of the 'Great Game' itself, with 'eyeball to eyeball' in Germany replacing 'telescope to telescope' in the Hindu Kush. The 'seamen versus landsmen' scenario was readily translatable into any of the contemporary idioms of confrontation, such as NATO versus the Warsaw Pact, capitalism versus communism, West versus East, freedom versus totalitarianism. It could thus be used as another weapon in the reinforcement of the system of belief which postulated the completeness of that duality running through all aspects of human life, even through the very stones of the planet itself. In other words, the theory could be supportive of ideological confrontation, just as Short saw Mackinder's original intention as having been the justification of maritime imperialism.

A wider explanation of the continued vigour of Heartland thinking can be reached by reference to emotional criteria operating within contemporary perceptions of global realities. Just as in the past such geographical terms as 'Spanish Main', 'North-West Frontier' and 'Near East' came to evoke the presence of real or imagined terrors, so did 'Heartland' move from the rational towards the non-rational. Hooson was of the opinion that this 'geographically charmed sanctuary' had come to possess 'an almost mystical aura', while Walters saw it as having come to be regarded as a great fortress surrounded by the rampart of the Iron Curtain. 'The silent castle', he said, was epitomised by the Kremlin itself which 'loomed overpoweringly in the dark recesses of the mind'. Legg was equally evocative in his description of the Heartland of bygone ages filled with mystery and fear to those living beyond its confines.[23] Now there had been a return of the old apprehension cast in new terms. Such terms, in particular 'communism', were new emotional reinforcements of a much older idea. In many ways they represented restatements in the contemporary idiom of that fear mingled with wonderment engendered by the great Heartland shining white and enormous in the light of the moon, as Mackinder had visualised it over half a century earlier.

The prolonged re-examination and re-evaluation of the Heartland concept in the context of the international situation in the aftermath of World War II helped provide the intellectual underpinning for the Cold War. Joseph Goebbels, Nazi Propaganda Minister, had in the last stages of the war foreseen the possibility of a confrontation between the Western allies and the Soviet Union.[24] It was this which had given him, and other leaders of the Third Reich, one last forlorn hope of survival. Goebbels used the term 'Iron Curtain' to describe the junction of the two great geopolitical blocs which he saw as about to inherit the territory of a prostrate Europe. In February 1946 the term was used by Churchill at a speech in Fulton, Missouri, when he warned of the dangers which now confronted the West.[25] The cold war between America and Russia was actually precipitated by the Greek civil war and the danger to that country's independence apparently emanating from the Soviets and their satellites. Britain's resources were at the time stretched to their limits, and the British government sought the aid of the United States in counteracting the communist threat both in

Greece and elsewhere in the eastern Mediterranean. The American response was contained in the Truman Doctrine of February 1947 which pledged United States aid to friendly countries facing either outside attack or internal subversion and this had the effect of extending some of the features of the Monroe Doctrine to other parts of the world. It was this which really marked an end to what Bowman had termed 'limited liability' and the beginning of a permanent American involvement in world affairs. From then on, whatever else may have been happening in the world, the conflict was essentially between the United States and the Soviet Union.

Ernest Bevin, the British Foreign Secretary from 1945 to 1950, had been instrumental in encouraging this development. From the beginning Bevin had been highly suspicious of Soviet motives and a firm believer in collective defence. His reports to Cabinet and other writings show that a very definite world view underlay his political actions. In 1945 he saw the post-war world as coming to consist of what he termed 'three great Monroes'.[26] There was the Western Hemisphere dominated by the power of the United States which was engaged in attempting to extend its Monroe principle to the Far East and so to control China and Japan. Then there was the Soviet Union whose sphere was now extending 'from Lübeck to the Adriatic in the West and to Port Arthur in the East'. Finally there was Britain and her Commonwealth standing uneasily between the two. He widened this into the concept of a 'western empire' covering Africa, the Middle East and India and invoked French support in its defence. It was the fear of a post-war world increasingly dominated by the two superpowers which was behind the British insistence that France should be elevated to the ranks of the 'Big Three' so converting them into the 'Big Four'. Bevin had become increasingly fearful of Russian pressure in the Mediterranean and in the 'northern tier' of Middle Eastern states, in particular Turkey and Iran. He believed that the Russian plan was to transform the Mediterranean from a British into a Russian lake and thus to cut the British — or European — 'Monroe' in half. Following the communist take-over in Czechoslovakia in 1948 he expressed the opinion that the Soviets were engaged in steadily extending their hold over Europe and had similar ambitions in the Middle and Far East. In Mackinder-style language he expressed his conviction that 'physical control of the whole World-Island is what the Politbureau is aiming at — no less a thing than that'.[27] His response was to promote the creation of the Western bloc possessing sufficient strength to deter the Russians. The Brussels Treaty of March 1948 linked Britain, France and the three Benelux countries into a defensive alliance. Then in the following year the North Atlantic Treaty Organisation (NATO) was established and this committed the United States firmly to the defence of Western Europe. Linked to this was the Marshall Plan which resulted in the Organisation for European Economic Cooperation (OEEC) channelling massive American financial aid to Europe. Thus by the end of Bevin's term of office, his two Western 'Monroes' had moved much closer together while the rift between them and the Soviet 'Monroe' had become a chasm.

During the 1950s further alliances on the model of NATO were established in other parts of the non-communist world. The most important of these were the Baghdad Pact (CENTO) and the South-East Asia Treaty Organisation (SEATO), both inspired by the United States. The principle behind them was the 'containment' strategy which had been developed and refined by George Kennan of the State Department. Kennan had had a close association with the Soviet Union over a number of years and had served as ambassador in Moscow. His judgement on Soviet intentions was a hard one and he assumed a fundamental aggressiveness and tendency to expansion which he was convinced America should do all in her power to prevent. In Kennan, according to Daniel Yergin, 'the Presbyterian Elder wrestled with the Bismarckian geopolitician'.[28] Many political geographers have seen the Kennan strategy as having been based on the ideas of Spykman and indeed those of Mackinder himself. For him the old Russia, with all its barbarism and intolerance, was never far beneath the surface and he was convinced that Marxism was little more than a 'fig leaf' to give moral respectability to Russia's ambitions. In face of such a threat to America's national security the 'subjective boundaries', as Yergin called them, were pushed expansively outwards so as 'to encompass more and more geography', thereby acquiring yet more problems.[29] This policy was implemented during the tenure of the State Department by John Foster Dulles, a firm and puritanical believer in American righteousness and in her duty to uphold her values throughout the world. The rim of Eurasia, from Scandinavia to the Philippines, was thus enmeshed with a system of military and political alliances in a manner which would certainly have been approved of by Bevin had he lived. The American post-war occupation of Japan was also subsequently to be converted into a close alliance between the two countries. The Eisenhower Doctrine of January 1957, promising further American military and financial aid to countries endangered by communist penetration, represented a further extension of Monroe-Truman thinking into the Middle Eastern region.

The Korean War which took place from 1950 to 1953 could be interpreted geopolitically as having been a classic struggle of land power against sea power. Supporters of the 'containment' strategy felt euphoric about its outcome since communist aggression had been held so effectively in check by the forces of the United Nations. Indeed both the maritime and the continental worlds were never more united within themselves than at that particular time. The two rival superpowers assumed the roles of champion of their particular causes and containment, confrontation and intervention became the watchwords of America's foreign policy.

The Americans had by the 1950s returned in effect to a Mercator-based world view but with one substantial difference: America was now firmly at the centre. In this American view, their country was, in A.K. Henrikson's phrase, an *insula fortunata* surrounded by wide oceans and willingly engaged in the Herculean task of shoring up the maritime peripheries. This task was, however, to prove beyond the resources of even this Hercules among the modern nations and, in any case, its geopolitical advisability was to be increasingly called into question.

'We must be careful not to be caught napping in the nineteenth century,' wrote Weigert in 1957.[30] He might also have observed that we should take care not to be discovered frozen in the cold war. Already by the late 1950s there were early signs that the rigid bipolar confrontation of the previous decade was about to be relaxed. With Stalin dead, the Soviet 'satellites' restive, China dissatisfied and the maritime empires fast disintegrating, massive changes were in train which were to transform the world in the 1960s. These were subsequently reflected in new directions of geopolitical thought.

Notes

1. R. Hartshorne, 'Political Geography' in P.E. James and C.F. Jones (eds.), *American Geography: Inventory and Prospect* (Association of American Geographers, Syracuse, 1954).

2. R. Muir, *Modern Political Geography* (Macmillan, London, 1975).

3. S.B. Jones, 'Views of the Political World', *Geographical Review*, XLV, 3 (1955).

4. J.R. Short, *An Introduction to Political Geography* (Routledge and Kegan Paul, London, 1982).

5. B.W. Blouet, 'H.G. Wells and the Evolution of Some Geographical Concepts', *Area*, 9 (1977).

6. W.H. Parker, *Mackinder: Geography as an Aid to Statecraft* (Clarendon, Oxford, 1982).

7. H.J. Mackinder, 'The Physical Basis of Political Geography', *Scottish Geographical Magazine*, 6 (1890).

8. E.W. Gilbert and W.H. Parker 'Mackinder's *Democratic Ideals and Reality* after Fifty Years', *Geographical Journal*, CXXXV, 2 (1969).

9. H.J. Mackinder, 'The Round World and the Winning of the Peace', *Foreign Affairs*, XXI, 4 (1943).

10. R.E. Walters, *The Nuclear Trap : An Escape Route* (Penguin, Harmondsworth, 1974).

11. N.J. Spykman, *The Geography of the Peace* (Harcourt Brace, New York, 1944).

12. H.W. Weigert, 'Heartland Revisited' in H.W. Weigert, V. Stefansson and R.E. Harrison (eds.), *New Compass of the World* (Macmillan, New York, 1949).

13. G.T. Renner, 'Maps for a New World', *Colliers Magazine*, CIX, 25 (1942).

14. Jones, 'Views of the Political World'.

15. G.B. Cressey, *Asia's Lands and Peoples* (McGraw Hill, New York, 1944).

16. G.B. Cressey, *The Basis of Soviet Strength* (McGraw Hill, New York, 1945).

17. C.B. Fawcett, 'Marginal and Interior Lands of the Old World' in H.W. Weigert *et al.*, *New Compass of the World*.

18. D.W. Meinig, 'Heartland and Rimland in Eurasian History', *Western Political Quarterly*, 9 (1956).

19. N.J.G. Pounds, *Political Geography* (McGraw Hill, New York, 1963).

20. D.J.M. Hooson, 'A New Soviet Heartland?', *Geographical Journal*, CXXVIII, 1 (1962); Hooson, *A New Soviet Heartland?* (Van Nostrand, Princeton, 1964).

21. A.P. de Seversky, *Air Power : Key to Survival* (Herbert Jenkins, London, 1952).

22. D.J.M. Hooson, 'A New Soviet Heartland?'.

23. S. Legg, *The Heartland* (Secker and Warburg, London, 1970).

24. H. Trevor-Roper (ed.), *The Goebbels Diaries: The Last Days* (Secker and Warberg, London, 1978).

25. G. Parker, *A Political Geography of Community Europe* (Butterworth, London, 1983), Chapter 1, note 3.

26. A. Bullock, *Ernest Bevin: Foreign Secretary 1945–51*, (Heinemann, London, 1983), Chapter 5.

27. W.H. Parker, *Mackinder*, Chapter 7.

28. D. Yergin, *The Shattered Peace: The Origin of the Cold War and the National Security State* (André Deutsch, London, 1978).

29. Ibid.

30. H.W. Weigert *et al.*, *Principles of Political Geography* (Appleton-Century-Crofts, New York, 1957).

9 A WORLD FRAGMENTED: GEOPOLITICS IN THE 1960s AND 1970s

The modified Heartland theories were attempts to construct a global system appropriate to the new circumstances after World War II. They represented attempts to build a theoretical framework for the new world order, using the bricks and mortar of the older theories. The object was to adapt and strengthen them, so enabling them to withstand the international seismic shocks to which the world had been subjected. However, by the end of the 1950s circumstances were producing a host of new geopolitical ideas, many of which eschewed the great systems in favour of a world of smaller units.

Such new ideas began to emerge just as the tight bipolar world appeared to be loosening up. East and Spate encapsulated this when they observed that 'it seems that a Communist bloc might not be so monolithic in practice as in theory'.[1] There was also a widespread and growing body of opinion which held that the bipolar world had been abnormal, born out of the special conditions and great uncertainties of the immediate post-war years. With the coming of more stable world conditions, the establishment of more permanent geopolitical structures could be anticipated.

The most spectacular changes in the world scene were coming in the wake of the final disintegration of the Eurocentric world order. Many of the host of newly independent countries which emerged as a result had little inclination to be automatically absorbed into the bipolar world system. Viewing both poles with some suspicion, they were more concerned to fulfil their own national destinies, but since most of them were small and weak they had to think in terms of co-operation both with their neighbours and with the great powers. There was thus need for the development of organisations at higher levels than those of the sovereign states which by the end of the 1950s were proliferating as never before. One of the answers to this situation and its inadequacy to meet the needs of the world at the time was the attempt to develop regional co-operation. The nature of this co-operation varied greatly, ranging from limited arrangements among former colonial territories to large groupings based upon cultural and political affinities. A number of political geographers studied this situation, attempting to explain it and to give it some sort of theoretical foundation.

A significant contribution to regionalist thinking was that of Saul Cohen in 1964.[2] Cohen accepted the divided world as a reality with which mankind had to live, being of the opinion that the object should be to make it as stable as possible. He considered that the development of regionalism was a hopeful sign for future stability. He rejected rigid world systems which gave little room for manoeuvre, considering rather that flexibility needed to be introduced into the concept. The Spykman-Kennan theses on the necessity for tight containment of the Eurasian-communist world were also rejected as being unrealistic. Quite apart from the question of its desirability or otherwise, the fact was that containment had not worked and that the maritime ring had frequently been either penetrated or leapfrogged by the Soviet Union. Along with others, Cohen was of the opinion that Heartland-Rimland thinking had made the Western world the victim of a myth about the strategy and tactics of global confrontation with the Soviet Union. This had resulted in what he called 'a frenzy of effort to plug all possible leaks in the Rimland dyke'.[3] When the achievement of this proved impossible, it became necessary to devise a more flexible response to the situation. Such flexibility was inherent in Cohen's grand design for a world of regions.

He distinguished two types of world regions, namely the geostrategic and the geopolitical. In the former category were the Trade-Dependent Maritime World and the Eurasian Continental World. There was also the possibility of the development of a third one, the Indian Ocean Plateau realm which he predicted would arise from the ashes of the British Commonwealth. The two great geostrategic regions were made up of a number of smaller geopolitical ones. Those constituting the Maritime World were Anglo-America and the Caribbean, Maritime Europe and the Maghreb, South America, Africa south of the Sahara and finally Off-Shore Asia and Oceania. The Continental World consisted of only two geopolitical regions, namely the Heartland, together with Eastern Europe, and East Asia (Figure 9.1). Each geopolitical region consisted either of one large state or of a group of smaller states, but the actual boundaries need not correspond with specific frontiers. Thus the southern boundary of Maritime Europe and Maghreb was to cut through the Sahara, while Anglo-America and the

Caribbean included parts of South America. Each of the geo-political regions had its own political, economic, social and cultural characteristics which gave it cohesion and which provided the *raison d'être* for unification. Each was also possessed of its own internal geopolitical structure, with an ecumene and a hinterland. The ecumene was the major centre of population and economic activity while the hinterland was a source of raw materials and could be an area for future development. These features were most in evidence in the most highly developed areas, such as Anglo-America, Maritime Europe and the Soviet Union, while in the least developed they had yet to appear. Cohen regarded the pro-cess of the unification of Europe as being the emergence of a new type of superstate. Maghreb he considered to be vital to it, other-wise Europe would be all ecumene and no hinterland. He identi-fied the principal power core of Anglo-America as being in the North-Eastern United States, whilst that of Eastern Europe-Heartland was in European Russia (Figure 9.2).

Separating the two geostrategic regions were the 'shatter-belts' of the Middle East and South-East Asia. Both had recently emerged from the colonial period, but both had failed to achieve the wider regional unity to which they aspired. Cohen attributed this unsatisfactory situation to internal physical divisions, to the absence of unitary geopolitical cores, and to the persistent external pressures emanating from both the Maritime and Continental geostrategic regions. Nationalist movements — Pan-Arab national-ism in particular — were seen as being basically a revolt against the conditions responsible for the instability which had made these regions into shatter-belts.

Cohen stated his aim as being 'to present a framework that anticipates the geographic dynamism of our times'.[4] Much of this dynamism was associated with the development of the strength of the geopolitical regions. One of these, Maritime Europe, was in course of becoming a centre of world power comparable with the two superpowers themselves. To him change was the salient feature, and the United States had to accept this fact and work to promote its own interests within it.

Nine years later Cohen again addressed himself to the problems of a 'World Divided'.[5] By then his opinion was that the loss of international purpose and the confusion in America's foreign policy were in large part the legacy of the containment strategy and the domino theory. His assessment was that America had become

Figure 9.1: Geopolitical and Geostrategic Regions of the World

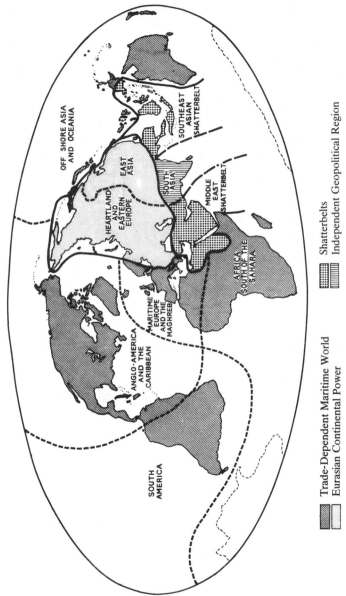

OFF SHORE ASIA AND OCEANIA

SOUTHEAST ASIAN SHATTERBELT

EAST ASIA

SOUTH ASIA

MIDDLE EAST SHATTERBELT

HEARTLAND AND EASTERN EUROPE

AFRICA SOUTH OF THE SAHARA

MARITIME EUROPE AND THE MAGHREB

ANGLO-AMERICA AND THE CARIBBEAN

SOUTH AMERICA

Trade-Dependent Maritime World
Eurasian Continental Power

Shatterbelts
Independent Geopolitical Region

Source: Cohen, S.B., *Geography and Politics in a Divided World* (Methuen, London, 1964).

Figure 9.2: The Major Geopolitical Regions and their Power Cores

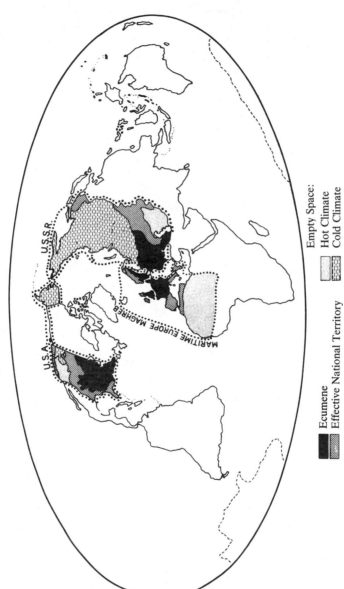

Ecumene

Effective National Territory

Empty Space:

Hot Climate

Cold Climate

Source: As in Figure 9.1.

'unglued', but he stressed his belief that coexistence was not just possible but essential if the world were to survive: 'The major premise of this work is that the dynamic balance that characterises relations among estates and larger regions is inherent in the ecology of the global political system.' This system was now seen as being a polycentric one possessed of four major power nodes. These were the United States, Maritime Europe, the Soviet Union and China. Although he recognised the greatly increased significance of the latter, now broken away from the Soviet Union, the two communist superpowers remained grouped together into a single geostrategic region, and the two geostrategic regions remained as previously delineated. Within this overall framework, he regarded a multiplicity of world power cores as being a better guarantee of global equilibrium than had been the bipolar world.

Crone in 1967 also outlined a hierarchical structure in which the smaller and more cohesive units nested in the larger and more amorphous.[6] The latter he referred to as being the two 'giant groups', and these had now been joined by a third group consisting in the main of newly independent tropical countries which had endeavoured to remain independent of either of the other two groups. Within this overall framework he identified at least ten large political groups of countries each forming units 'which themselves have an historic justification or a cultural basis'.[7] Among them he included the Soviet bloc, Western Europe, the Arab world, Black Africa, India and South-East Asia. He was of the opinion that what had triggered off the transformation from bipolar to multipolar had been the emergence of China as a fully independent world power. This event had been all the more significant since Chinese policy was dedicated at the time to the destruction of capitalism and neo-colonialism, thus making the country into a potential leader of the Afro-Asian nations.

In the same year de Blij[8] identified 'major trends' in the global scene, one of the most significant of these in his view being regionalism. He considered the five most significant ideological-ethnic regions as being the West, the Soviet bloc, China, the Arab world and Africa. Each of these had been developing increasing cohesiveness and this was a tendency which was likely to continue. The most important of the states not included in any of these regions were located in Southern Asia, and de Blij foresaw the possibility of a sixth world region eventually emerging there. He was not, however, one of those who entirely welcomed this regionalism.

'We can observe the intensification of the divisive functions of certain boundaries and their reduction in others,' he commented.[9]

Other significant developments observed by de Blij in 1967 were the rise of China, the eastward movement of the Soviet power core and the emergence of the Pacific as a major centre of geopolitical activity. China was the first really effective challenge to the white races from the non-white, since she was potentially a far more significant power than had been Japan. In view of the Soviet Union's move into Asia, this challenge would in the first instance be directed against her. This was one of the factors in the new role of the Pacific in world affairs, since, according to de Blij, 'with the rise of China to world power, the Pacific has taken on the role history also allotted to the Mediterranean and later the Atlantic: adversaries face each other across its waters'. There are echoes of Haushofer in his assertion that the future of the politico-geographical world may well be determined in the Pacific.

Russett employed quantitative techniques in order to examine the realities behind the growth of regionalism.[10] Using factor analysis of 54 separate variables he discovered enough correlations to enable him to identify clustering into groups. On the basis of congruence in socio-cultural homogeneity and political and economic interdependence, the regional groupings which most clearly emerged were the Western Community, Afro-Asia, Latin America and Eastern Europe. On the basis of his findings he was able to predict a continuation of integrative trends at regional levels, but since national systems were themselves so strongly entrenched, he was of the opinion that the emergence of regional groupings was likely to be a slow process. Like de Blij, he did not regard regionalism as being an unmitigated blessing, since conflict could take place among such units as easily as it had done among nation states. It would all depend on how the new system was used, since it had the potential for being either 'a stable political edifice for man or merely a shaky temple he can pull down upon his head'.

Cantori and Spiegel were of the opinion that since not all world events relate directly to the confrontation of the superpowers, regionalism could provide 'a missing link in the chain of explanation'.[11] They saw a world with three hierarchical systems, the dominant, subordinate and internal. The dominant system consisted of the global arena in which the major great power relationships took place. The subordinate systems were the regions which were the interactive fields of contiguous groups of states.

The internal systems consisted of the totality of affairs within individual states. Each system had its own spatial character with a core and a periphery. The core of each international system consisted of those countries or areas which were the focuses of activity within the system and around which it had developed. The periphery was made up of countries and areas less directly involved in the affairs of the region, but which nevertheless were attracted towards it.

The dominant system consisted of three great powers — the United States, the Soviet Union and China — and they were deemed to be the only really global international actors. The subordinate systems were five in number, these being Latin America, West Africa, the Middle East, Western Europe and South-East Asia. Each of these fulfilled the role of a system as a result of the interaction of 'four pattern variables', these being levels of internal cohesion, the communications networks, levels of power and the structure of relationships. Cutting across this hierarchy there were also the intrusive systems in which the more powerful countries sought influence outside their own regions by organising frameworks of action. The five powers capable of managing such systems were considered to be the United States, the Soviet Union, China, France and Great Britain. The Organisation of American States, the British Commonwealth and the French Community are examples of international groupings brought about in this way.

A number of American political scientists, notably Haas, Deutsch and Etzioni, also studied the process of regional integration and theorised on the optimum conditions for its achievement. These were found to depend upon a whole range of spatial, political, social and economic factors. Etzioni believed that continuous territory and a morphology suitable to intra-regional communication were vital.[12] 'Ecological unity' was a fundamental necessity, and if the unity of the ecological base were to be broken by a 'no-man's-land' or by the interposition of non-member states, such discontinuity would be unsettling and produce tensions. Haas talked of the 'logic of integration' given optimum conditions, and these included the presence of a regional core possessed of sufficient power to encourage the rest of the region to coalesce around it.[13] There also needed to be adequate communication structures to facilitate high levels of internal transactions at various levels. The conditions of regional 'take-off' were the existence of 'sympathy feelings' among the national élites, mutually compatible political systems and widespread popular expectations of the advantages to be derived from integration. The principal catalysts of regional integration, according to Nye, could be both indigenous and external.[14] The principal external one was likely to be a threat to the group as a whole. The internal ones could be either the common expectation of advantage, or else coercion by one of the region's member states. This latter he referred to as 'the Bismarckian method'.

As an antidote to excessive euphoria regarding the triumph of regionalism, Hansen drew attention to the continuing strength of nationalism.[15] Parallel to the 'logic of integration' there was also a 'logic of diversity', since the nation-state remained the most developed and successful form of political organisation over much of the world. Dikshit saw an answer to this apparent conflict of centripetal and centrifugal tendencies in the institution of federation.[16] This allowed 'regionally grouped diversities' to be incorporated into convenient geographical units. Political evolution could then take place at a speed appropriate to local conditions so that 'the units merge only when the centripetal forces overwhelm the separatist ones, and the units see greater advantages in union than in separation'.

The marked emphasis on the theory and practice of regional integration arose both from the end of the European world empires and from a search for an alternative to the sterile and dangerous dichotomy of the two superpowers. While there were considerable differences in interpretation and emphasis, there were also certain common approaches to the whole matter. Regionalism was seen as a process whereby territorial units consisting of a number of contiguous nation-states possessing similar physical and human characteristics were in course of development. The whole process was to be observed in many parts of the world, but, while quite advanced in some areas, in others it was barely discernible at all. The impulses towards integration were of many sorts and each region tended to possess its own particular combination, but the most successful regions had developed around multinational cores which provided the dynamic for further expansion and integration of the group.

Furthermore there was a widespread acceptance of the concept of a hierarchical global structure in which regional systems could be seen in the context of others operating both above and below them. There was, however, no such agreement on the actual or potential relationship between the regional and the higher or global systems. There were those who saw the new regional group-ings as having a relatively fixed and subordinate position in the world system as a whole. Others envisaged the world situation as a far more fluid one in which future changes in alliance patterns and shifts in the balance of power could be expected to produce radical changes on the world scene.

The most impressive manifestations of the new regionalism were located in the Northern Hemisphere, and it was here also that the great centres of world power were to be found. This led to the problem of the relationship of regional groupings to the great powers and in particular to the superpowers themselves. The central question was whether the superpowers were the repositories of overwhelming international power and as such unchallengable into the foreseeable future, or whether some of the new regions were themselves superpowers in the making which would inevitably alter the world scene as they evolved further. This in turn relates to wider perceptions of the development of the international scene.

There appears to have been almost general agreement among political geographers that the principal catalyst for the trans-formation of the world geopolitical scene was the emergence of China as a great power in its own right. From then on it no longer accorded with the facts to equate communism with a massive and menacing Eurasian bloc poised ready to make Mackinder's dire warnings come true. Nor was it realistic to justify the bipolar world as being an inevitable and natural development consequent upon the whittling down in the numbers of great powers during the present century. Apparently the process had gone into reverse, and it was consequently necessary to think out the geopolitical implica-tions of this. A similar crack in the Western alliance with Maritime Europe, and in particular the European Community, engaged in creating its own tighter supra-national structures, suggested that this was not merely a temporary aberration. The most convincing explanation of both these developments was that power was now beginning to spread to new centres, and consequently a multipolar world system was beginning to emerge.

Kaplan had been among the first to understand these develop-ments and to put them into the context of a model of changing international power structures.[17] He saw the global balance of power at any period as being the result of the interaction of a com-plex of variables. The continued existence of this global balance was dependent upon the continuation of this same set of variables, and when these ceased to operate then the existing system would be replaced by another more responsive to the new conditions. He referred to the late 1950s as having a 'loose bi-polar system' in which change was constrained by a combination of the concentration of global power and the nuclear threat. The imminent arrival of China on the scene heralded the 'tri-polar' world system and this would be followed by a 'multi-polar' system with Western Europe and Japan added. The new system would require a change in the rules of international behaviour to make it operate more like the balance of power in the nineteenth century.

The multipolar theory, however, was in practice not widely accepted because of the overwhelming preponderance of the two superpowers as contrasted with the hesitant and limited moves towards regional integration elsewhere. It was the necessity of incorporating the superpowers into the system which was basic to the concept of hierarchy. This certainly appeared to be a truer representation of the realities of the world geopolitical scene in the 1960s. The concept also had the advantage of stimulating a belief in the feasibility of coexistence between the two ideologically opposed systems. This could be achieved through Cohen's global balance which introduced a reassuring stability into an otherwise rapidly changing and potentially chaotic situation. His 'isostatic balance of power' was not rigid but allowed for movement and adjustment; even the Soviet Union appeared in a rather more benign light than previously and began to take on the role of a force for world stability.

East, de Blij and Crone were among those who also pointed to a more basic shift in the world power balance away from Europe and the West and towards Asia and the Pacific. With the Soviet Union becoming more an Asiatic power and America more Pacific than Atlantic oriented, it was thus here that the great confrontations of the future would, in their view, be likely to take place. Certainly in this arena the Soviet Union, China and the United States were deemed likely to remain the major protagonists for some time into the future.

The breakdown of post-war world geopolitical structures during the 1960s and 1970s was in practice brought about by the re-emergence of two important political ideas. These ideas were nationalism and internationalism, and the impact of both on the world scene proved to be considerable. Protagonists of the former included such figures as Charles de Gaulle and Mao Zedong, and of the latter Jean Monnet, Robert Schuman and Third World leaders such as Nasser and Nehru. De Gaulle had always been a firm believer in the *grandeur* of France, and had maintained that France was either great or she was nothing. He completely refused to accept the view of the maritime world which emanated from Britain and America. His wartime experiences had led him to believe that *les anglo-saxons* wished only to entrench their own dominant positions, and was determined that France should in no way be a part of this. Consequently during the 1960s France left the military arm of NATO, American forces were removed from French soil and the country's independent nuclear arsenal was strengthened. Closer relations were cultivated with the Soviet Union and encouragement was given to the development of a more independent European stance in foreign policy. This *stratégie tous azimuths* aimed at making France an independent world power between the two superpowers although in practice the country remained nearer to the West than to the Soviets. It was a position strikingly similar to that envisaged for Britain by Bevin in the years immediately following World War II but which had been largely abandoned during the 1950s. At around the same time Mao was withdrawing from the tightly-drawn communist bloc in which he found the Soviet Union to be unacceptably dominant. He took literally the Lenin dictum 'national in form and socialist in content', and during the 1960s moved China to a position of complete independence from Moscow. This also represented a return towards the old Sinocentric world view and a willingness to enter into relations with countries of whatever ideological persuasion so long as this appeared to be in China's national interest. This proved to be a more realistic long-term course of action for China with its enormous territory and population than for France which was far smaller and geographically embedded in Western Europe. Under de Gaulle's successors France moved slowly but surely back into the Western camp.

Regional forms of internationalism developed fastest in Western Europe during the 1950s. The autarchic nationalism of the 1930s was seen to have led to disaster and in the aftermath of World War II international co-operation appeared to be the only realistic path to follow. Jean Monnet's principle was that the finding of solutions to particular questions would inevitably lead to the development of wider institutions of international co-operation. This was the 'functional' principle behind the European Coal and Steel Community (ECSC) which he and the French Foreign Minister, Robert Schuman, steered successfully through the minefield of national suspicions. It was followed in 1957 by the European Economic Community (EEC) which broadened the sphere of co-operation, established the principle of supranationalism, and introduced a basis for future political co-operation. The Community idea represented a new approach to the satisfaction of French economic and security needs. It contained many of the ideas which had been formulated by French political geographers, in particular Demangeon, during the years before the war. These had influenced French 'Europeans' such as Briand who in turn were to influence the generation of 'Europeans' of the 1950s (see Chapter 6).

By the late 1950s France had moved into a dominating position in European affairs, but her neighbour Germany had remained totally crushed for many years following the end of the war. The Iron Curtain, foreseen by Goebbels in the smoking ruins of his Propaganda Ministry, cut right through her territory and the division of the world was mirrored in microcrosm on her soil. *Mitteleuropa* as a geopolitical concept had completely disappeared and been replaced by an iron line of confrontation. The *détente* atmosphere in the 1960s encouraged attempts to bring back some semblance of international normality to the continent and this hinged on German acceptance of the post-war status quo. The matter was skilfully handled by Willy Brandt, Foreign Minister and later Chancellor of the German Federal Republic. His *Ostpolitik* culminated in 1972 in treaties with both Poland and the Soviet Union in which the Federal Republic accepted the Eastern European situation. He was thus able to inaugurate a new era of improved relations without in any way departing from his country's close ties with the West or altering fundamentally the 'two Europes' which had existed since the 1940s.

Meanwhile America was coming to terms with yet another 'New World', at least the third major international scene change since Bowman had originally used the phrase. By the 1960s her role in the Western alliance had become a decidedly more modest one than it had been in the decade and a half after World War II. Kennedy, who was President between 1960 and 1963, welcomed Europe's new strength and talked of a partnership of equals between the two sides of the Atlantic. The idea of the Atlantic as being an 'inland sea' in the words of Walter Lippmann, the

American political commentator, was reminiscent of Mackinder's 'Midland Ocean' and implied the unity of the 'Atlantic system' as a whole. The Atlantic was seen as continuing to narrow and there were even suggestions of an 'Atlantic Community' on the model of EEC so as to strengthen NATO. Although President Nixon himself remained highly conscious of the continuing need for close Western co-operation, the foreign policy of the Nixon administration from 1969 to 1974 was far less emotionally tied to Europe. Secretary of State Henry Kissinger viewed American interests in a very different way and with far greater fluidity. He saw the world as being increasingly dominated by a pentarchy of great powers, these being the United States, the Soviet Union, Europe, China and Japan. It was therefore necessary to construct a world balance of power on the model of the European balance which had existed before World War I. This 'pentagonalism' implied an abandonment of the fixed positions of the 'containment' era and an end to the acceptance of the world view upon which they had been founded. The Kissinger world view was thus close to Kaplan's theory of a 'multipolar' system and required substantial changes in international behaviour to ensure its smooth operation. It implied mobility, incorporating flexible positions and allowing for something like Cohen's isostatic changes to take place. The pentagonal view of the world had also the effect of further entrenching the dominance of the Northern Hemisphere and particularly of that 'Northern Belt' which had been postulated by Fairgrieve half a century earlier during World War I.

It was thinking along these lines which eventually led to the *détente* in superpower relations which took place in the late 1960s. This was accompanied by economic and cultural agreements between the two powers, negotiations on arms control and the signature in 1972 of the SALT I agreement on nuclear weapons limitations. The long Vietnam War, fought in obedience to the now largely discredited principles of 'containment', came to an inglorious end in the following year. Of even greater moment was the improvement in relations with China which since the communist take-over in 1949 had been dubbed an international pariah. In 1972 President Nixon made his notable state visit to China and, after a quarter-century of semi-isolation, the country was at last brought back into the international community. In the Kissinger world view, the great power of the Orient also became a possible international counterweight to the Soviet Union. This further added to its attractions for Nixon who, as a veteran cold warrior, remained wary of his old antagonist. There were many other political leaders on both sides of the Atlantic who shared these feelings. Behind the Iron Curtain the Romanians discovered a new freedom of action by playing the China card, and to the Albanians China at first appeared to be the perfect patron for a small state. The spectre of the cold war thus continued to haunt the feast even in the brave new world of international *détente* and fluidity.

Notes

1. W.G. East and O.H.K. Spate, 'Epilogue: The Unity of Asia?' in *The Changing Map of Asia* (Harrap, London, 1961).
2. S.B. Cohen, *Geography and Politics in a Divided World* (Methuen, London 1964).
3. Ibid., Chapter 3.
4. Ibid., Conclusion.
5. S.B. Cohen, *Geography and Politics in a World Divided* (Oxford University Press, 1973).
6. G.R. Crone, *Background to Political Geography* (Pitman, London, 1967).
7. Ibid.
8. H.J. de Blij, *Systematic Political Geography* (John Wiley, New York, 1967).
9. Ibid., Chapter 7.
10. B.M. Russett, *International Regions and the International System: A Study in Political Ecology* (Chicago, 1967).
11. L.J. Cantori and S.L. Spiegel, *The International Politics of Regions* (Prentice-Hall, Englewood Cliffs, New Jersey, 1970).
12. A. Etzioni, 'A Paradigm for the Study of Political Unification' in R. E. Kasperson and J.V. Minghi (eds.), *The Structure of Political Geography* (University of London Press, London, 1970).
13. E.B. Haas, 'The Challenge of Regionalism' in W.A.D. Jackson and M.S. Samuels (eds.), *Politics and Geographic Relationships* (Prentice-Hall, Englewood Cliffs, New Jersey, 1971); and Haas, 'International Integration: the European and the Universal Process' in E.M. Hodges (ed.), *European Integration* (Penguin, Harmondsworth, 1972).
14. J.S. Nye, 'Patterns and Catalysts in Regional Integration' in W.A.D. Jackson and M.S. Samuels (eds), *Politics and Geographic Relationships* (Prentice-Hall, Englewood Cliffs, New Jersey, 1971).
15. R. Hansen, 'Regional Integration: Reflections on a Decade of Theoretical Efforts' in E.M. Hodges (ed.), *European Integration* (Penguin, Harmondsworth, 1972).
16. R.D. Dikshit, *The Political Geography of Federalism: an Enquiry into Origins and Stability* (Macmillan, Delhi, 1975).
17. M.A. Kaplan, *Systems and Process in International Politics* (Wiley, New York, 1957).

10 THE EMPEROR'S NEW CLOTHES: RADICAL ALTERNATIVES IN CONTEMPORARY THOUGHT

During the 1970s a great change was taking place in geographical thinking, one of the main features of which was the establishment of viable and radical alternatives to the conventional wisdoms of the subject. It was founded on a growing conviction that while geographers had learned to study mankind with ever greater sophistication, man himself had been largely lost in the process. As Busteed put it: 'Too many geographers have loved humanity but could not stand people.'[1] The new attitudes were eloquently expressed in *Humanistic Geography*[2] edited by Ley and Samuels and in *Radical Geography*[3] edited by Peet. The social sciences, said Ley and Samuels, had successfully broken down man for the purposes of study into specialist compartments but 'as with Humpty Dumpty, not all the methodological weapons at their command could put him together again'.[4] The principal task for geographers, then, was to strive to comprehend the world and the interrelationships of the various phenomena which combine to make it up. It was a kind of new renaissance in which man, the measure of all things, was once more to be restored to wholeness.

Another element in the change was the rebellion by younger geographers against what they alleged to have been the role of orthodox geography in the past as justifier of capitalism, militarism, imperialism and the oppression of the poor by the rich. If the subject were to be able to address itself more effectively to the world's problems, then it would be necessary to replace comfortable establishment geography with one with a more powerful social cutting edge. Issues considered worthy of critical examination by the new breed of geographers included the nuclear question, the plight of the world's poor, the dangers of conflict and, above all, the potentially disastrous consequences for 'planet earth' of the unrestricted and competitive exploitation of its finite resources and of tampering with its fragile ecosystem. The oil crisis of 1973, which triggered the general crisis of the 1970s, made these dangers all too real and provided a menacing backdrop to the search for radical alternatives.

This new radical humanism in geography had important consequences for the direction of geopolitical thought. Of particular significance was the reappraisal of Marxism and the attempt to give
Marxian thinking a spatial perspective. This is particularly associated with Harvey who stated that revolutionary theory in geography should be grounded in the reality which it seeks to present.[5]
It should aim to understand the dialectical interaction between
social process and spatial form and so offer real choices for the
future of the social process. He analysed the geography of
capitalism and showed how the capitalist concentration of wealth
and power implied the necessity to annihilate space by time. This
resulted in agglomeration into a number of large centres which
became the workshops of capitalist production. The concentration
of capital into the hands of the few was thus accompanied by a
parallel geographical concentration of labour and fixed capital.
According to Harvey, 'capital thus comes to represent itself in the
form of a physical landscape created in its own image'. This is
either its 'crowning glory' or 'a prison which inhibits the further
progress of accumulation'. The result is a perpetual struggle in
which the 'long wave' crises of capitalism necessitate a periodic
reshaping of the geographical environment. In the capitalist landscape there is thus tension and contradiction rather than har-
monious equilibrium. As Marx himself said, this results in special-
isation and division and so 'converts one part of the globe into a
chiefly agricultural field of production for supplying the other part
which remains as chiefly industrial fields'. As interdependence
grows, so non-capitalist modes of production will be destroyed and
former colonial territories will eventually themselves become
centres of capitalist power and accumulation. A tendency to continued expansion is another feature inherent in capitalism, and this
will cause its continued territorial extension. Yet Marx also saw
capitalism as being a civilising influence in the world, bringing
about the replacement of local and primitive societies by more
advanced ones. This all led in the direction of a world society
which would replace the previous local and largely independent
ones. However, the contradictions in capitalism made this uni-
versality unattainable in practice and instead it would eventually
move towards its own suspension. Marx did not himself produce a
theory of the relationship of capitalism to imperialism, but Lenin
viewed imperialism as being the final stage of capitalism arising out
of the dialectics of capitalist accumulation. Imperialist war would

eventually lead to the final and violent end of the capitalist era.

Nevertheless, viewed in the context of geographical realities, Marxian theory demonstrated to Harvey that capitalism had in fact been the vehicle for the atomisation of the world, and it could only be made whole again by the replacement of capitalism by co-operative structures. Here Marxian geographers turned back to the ideas of Kropotkin[6] and Reclus[7] on the essential unity of man and nature and the historical tendency towards co-operation. It was such beliefs as this which justified the hope that the capitalist landscape with its disequilibrium could be replaced by a new one of equilibrium and harmony.

Quaini's examination revealed the profound differences between capitalist and pre-capitalist societies and the spatial implications of this.[8] He demonstrated that Marx had been overly historical in his approach, and had shown little real sense of the role which spatial variations could play. There was need to rectify this, since a knowledge of the nature of space was essential in order to be able to transform society. Quaini rejected orthodox geographical perspectives and, drawing on Ferrier, Racine and Raffestin,[9] proposed a 'critical paradigm' for the construction of 'a model of the geo-historical reality of its time'.

The application of Marxian principles to dynamic spatial thinking was also seen to provide a revolutionary conceptual framework for the diachronic analysis of economic processes. This was turned by Wallerstein into a model of world politico-economic development.[10] He maintained that the global totality was now the only really effective unit of study in the social sciences, since individual states and separate processes could not any longer be fully comprehended outside their wider context. He identified three basic types of society, the reciprocal-lineage mode, the world empires and the world economy. This latter was capitalist, but unlike the world empires did not possess an overall political structure. It had spread widely over the earth's surface, absorbed the contemporary world empires and created what was, in effect, a single world unit. This expanding capitalist world economy operated with two fundamental inequalities: the class inequality of bourgeois and proletariat, and the spatial inequality of core and periphery. Politico-economic structures were periodically adjusted in order to strengthen the system as a whole.

Wallerstein saw the pre-capitalist core has having originated in North-West Europe in the sixteenth century and having subsequently developed into a capitalist core centring on Great Britain. Around this centre a world periphery and semi-periphery then developed. In the present century the core expanded and hegemony passed to the United States. The core is now in Europe and North America and most of the rest of the world is periphery. The core possesses the highest levels of affluence and economic development, while the periphery has the greatest poverty and underdevelopment. The two are linked together by the capitalist world system as a whole and Wallerstein maintained that underdevelopment in the periphery is a direct consequence of capitalist penetration and peripheral status. Only the communist states have been able to withdraw from the capitalist world economy as a positive response to the dangers of peripheralisation. This they have achieved through the adoption of statist policies which Wallerstein sees as being a form of latter-day mercantilism.

The Wallersteinian world system has been criticised for claiming too much influence both for the European core and for the relationship of core and periphery in the development of capitalism. Nevertheless, it has come to be widely regarded as being a landmark in the application of Marxian ideas to the understanding of world politico-economic development. As such it has also been of considerable importance in the reorientation of geopolitical thought. Taylor encapsulated this when he expressed the opinion that

> Wallerstein's world-economy approach presents an opportunity for political geographers to return to the global scale of analysis without paying any homage to Mackinder. Whereas Mackinder points towards East versus West conflict (the basis of his continuing popularity) and hence intra-core conflict, the Wallerstein approach places the North versus South conflict at the centre of the stage.[11]

This interpretation turned the historic geopolitical orientation around by 180° and Modelski went on to relegate the intra-core conflict of the Northern Hemisphere to competition for global economic-monopoly rights.[12] This is in a way a reactivation of Lenin's theory of imperialism taking on board the developed communist societies as well. The whole concept was given full airing by Strassoldo, Claval, Henrikson and others in Gottmann's *Centre and Periphery*.[13] Strassoldo saw this global dichotomy deriving from Wallerstein as also echoing older ideas about centrality and territorial organisation.[14] However, he is critical of the concept as indicative of some sort of fixed or even final state, seeing continued flux and differentiation. He cites Toynbee on the interchangability of cores and peripheries and the way in which old periphery can become new core. The whole idea of periphery seems to him to derive from the current situation of a finite world which sets definite limits to further expansion. In the past 'periphery' had been 'frontier' which implied a differentiation or break rather than a terminus. It had been appropriate to the idea of an expanding world in which progress had occurred in an 'unilinear, infinite, evolutionary trajectory'. This had been the world view encapsulated in the phrase 'go west, young man' but the world was now a closed system and there was nowhere else to go. In such circumstances the world periphery at the edge of the system was endowed with negative rather than positive qualities and appeared as being chronically inferior to the centre. The frontier as outlet for human frustrations and hopes was replaced by periphery as boundary of human aspirations and possibilities. This situation was potentially highly unstable and carried considerable danger of an explosive reaction.

Strassoldo was thus of the opinion that it was the mood of the times which accounted for the popularity of notions of centre and periphery. He envisaged the possibility of this in time giving place to more positive and encouraging ideas. The grounds for this moderate optimism lay partly in the discrediting of the mystique of power associated with the glorification of the capital (centre) as a sacred notion: 'The emperor's clothes have been stripped to show his naked power.' There was still time for good sense to prevail and for mankind at last to learn to live socially in 'the global village' without hierarchies and their various spatial manifestations. 'It seems that the postindustrial, communicational, informational, techtronic, cybernetic society towards which our civilisation is moving ... has no major objection to the end of the centre-periphery duality,' he suggested.

Claval regarded the whole centre versus periphery dialectic as being over-simplistic, relying for its effect more on expressive imagery than coherent theory.[15] He saw it as more or less a spatial translation of Marxism, seeking to explain everything through 'the domination game'. Yet the hegemonic model inherent in it had effectively come to an end with the first Soviet nuclear test. The balance of terror thenceforth enabled peripheral powers to break the hegemonic patterns imposed upon them. Poles of power multiplied under the shadow of the bomb and a partial shift has already taken place towards the periphery. For Claval reliance on the centre-periphery dialectic risked hiding the deeper causes of the problems of the contemporary world.

Another French political geographer, Raffestin, touched on this question in his analysis of the geographical basis of power.[16] He was of the opinion that the imbalance contained a built-in self-regulating mechanism since the features of the spatial structures of the metropolitan powers tended to be reproduced by the colonies. As a result they eventually came to function in a very similar manner.

In his contribution to the centre-periphery arguments, Henrikson observed that since the reconstellation of global forces in the early 1940s in what amounted to a geopolitical 'Copernican Revolution', the United States had been the geostrategic centre of the world, a colossus with one foot in Europe and the other in Asia.[17] This situation had now come to an end, and the country's world position was in decline. Americans were consequently uncertain and apprehensive, fearing relegation to 'the political periphery of a postindustrial North'. Kissinger had attempted to come to terms with the new situation with his concept of a 'pentagonal' world (Figure 10.1). In this concept the United States was thus relegated from being the main centre of world power to being just one of a number of such centres. Underlying this new position was the profoundly altered world situation. Since the oil crisis, maintained Henrikson, there were few absolute and fixed positions and everywhere 'a sense of geopolitical flux' and a new relativity. Possible explanations of this could be sought in the related theories of 'diffusion of power' and 'polytectonic zones': according to the former, the economic and technological ingredients of power are becoming diffused throughout the world, and, as power gradients diminish, the West is losing its lead; the latter is a geological analogy suggesting a world of independent power blocs geopolitically 'floating' and consequently not tied to inherited groupings. Like Strassoldo, Henrikson retained an optimism about the world's future. This appeared to stem less from his thoughts about shifts in the balance of power than from the sense of danger confronting humanity. The very unity and vulnerability of 'spaceship earth' and its seeming uniqueness in the galaxy led him to the conclusion that

Figure 10.1: New Geometry for a Changing World. The triangular great power relationships fitted together into a 'quinquelateral' world order.

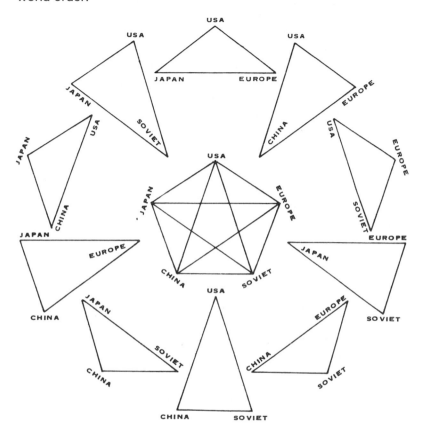

Source: Spiro, H.J., 'Interdependence: A Third Option Between Sovereignty and Supranational Integration', in Ionescu, G. (ed.) *Between Sovereignty and Integration.* (Croom Helm, London, 1974).

co-operative rather than destructive solutions must and will be sought.

Abdel-Malek implicitly accepted a centre-versus-periphery framework although he saw it as the dialectic of imperialism and the freedom of the new nations.[18] At Yalta the world had been organised for the benefit of the West, but this order of things was now in its final stages. He saw it as being brought to an end by the rise of the power of the Orient, and he quoted the Chinese thesis that 'East wind prevails over West wind'. He envisaged a world consisting of three great power groups. There would be an Eurasian bloc led by the Soviet Union; an Asian-Oriental bloc led by China in alliance with the Arabs and Japan and finally a Western-American bloc which would include Australasia, Southern Africa and Latin America. A duality emerged out of this triple order since there was a major contradiction between the blocs led by the two socialist powers and that led by the United States.

Brunn also accepted that the world scene had been subject to radical alteration during the 1970s.[19] Up to then there had been a 'dynamic equilibrium' in global geopolitics, but he saw 'the equilibriating forces ... themselves being altered'. He examined the changing world scene in the 1980s and attempted to identify its salient features. These included the emergence of a new international economic order, the growth of regional powers, and the importance of both transnational regional co-operation and of the transnational corporations (TNCs).

The new international economic order had its origin in the success of OPEC in demanding and getting more for their oil from the consuming countries which were vulnerable to the cutting off of oil supplies. This had encouraged the Third, Fourth and Fifth Worlds to demand greater shares, and a power shift was beginning to take place. As the nineteenth century had been dominated by Europe and the twentieth century by the superpowers, so in the next century it could be the turn of the Third World. There was evidence for this development in the rise of regional powers such as Nigeria, Saudi-Arabia, Iran, India and Brazil. Related to this there was the growing power of regionalist movements such as Islam and Pan-Africa. Among the forces ranged against this shift of economic and political power were the TNCs with their capital, technology and commercial skill. To Brunn they were a form of non-territorial imperialism emanating from the traditional centres of Western world power such as London, Paris and New York. The acquisition of 'real estate' in the old imperial manner was likely to take second place in future to ensuring supplies of foodstuffs, energy and physical resources.

Other contemporary political geographers stressed the important role of the TNCs. Glassner and de Blij[20] envisaged that they would in future exist in tandem with the territorial states. As a result of their flexibility and their relative freedom from territorial restraints they could well outlast many existing states. To Raffestin also, power in the modern world had a non-territorial dimension, in particular through the geopolitical implications of the financial system.[21] The deployment of finance capital was seen as being a kind of '*circulation souterrain*' emanating from epicentres in the West and moving largely undetected until its often destructive effects became apparent on the surface. This concept provided a sort of subterranean counterpart to Harvey's capitalist landscapes. However, Raffestin also saw the TNCs as potential agents for the diffusion of technology into the poorer world. Short, on the other hand, saw the Corporations as being threads linking the core to the periphery, channelling back profits into the core and in the process helping to reinforce underdevelopment.[22] Counter capital flows in the form of aid to the periphery were minute in both actual and relative terms, and often had the aggregate effect of exacerbating the problem of dependence.

Blaut summed up the whole composite North-South problem when he asserted that the successful tackling of the problems of the Third World necessitated a completely new view of global relationships, and in particular a psychological reorientation in the core.[23] Such a new geographical perspective 'redraws our mappa mundi; in fact offers an alternative historical atlas of the world since 1492'. An interesting attempt to achieve this cartographically is the Peters projection (Figure 10.2) which aims to replace the traditional emphasis on the northern world by a new emphasis on the southern world. Nevertheless, Blaut did perceive some hopeful signs of movement, particularly associated with OPEC and the emergence of the newly industrialising countries (NICs). These were now the most advanced parts of the South and had become areas of autocentric growth outside the core.

This new North-South orientation brought to the public attention by the Brandt Report,[24] together with the considerable social concern upon which it was based, meant that for a time rather less attention was given to the question of East-West relations in the global context. However, even if it could be relegated to the status of a subsystem, or some sort of 'cold' civil war in the rich world, it was there that the greatest and most frightening power still resided. Back in the early 1960s Cohen had criticised the domino theory, which in one form or another had underpinned American foreign policy since the early 1950s, for being not only wrong, but quite impracticable given the limits to America's power.[25] In 1982 he

Figure 10.2: The Poor World Shown on Peters' Projection. Arno Peters' decimal grid divides the surface of the Earth into 100 longitudinal fields of equal width and 100 latitudinal fields of equal height. The map is then built up from the Equator and so shows the world as viewed from a 'Southern' perspective.

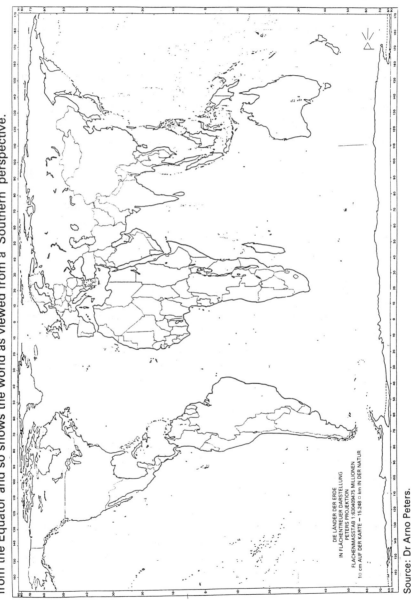

DIE LÄNDER DER ERDE
IN FLÄCHENTREUER DARSTELLUNG
PETERS PROJEKTION
FLÄCHENMASSTAB 1:630409475 MILLIONEN
1 cm AUF DER KARTE = 15.248 ☐ km IN DER NATUR

Source: Dr Arno Peters.

once more addressed himself to the problem of global geopolitical equilibrium.[26] His method was to apply the developmental approach in general systems theory to the contemporary geo-political situation. Through this he identified a process of spatial evolution from undifferentiated to specialised and then hier-archical structures. He saw in the 1980s all three stages in this process coexisting in a state of 'geopolitical disequilibrium'. In the transition from the previous state of international equilibrium towards a new one there was a Hegelian conflict and a search for the unification of opposites. Cohen saw the principal catalysts for change as being the second-order powers which had already narrowed the gap between themselves and the major powers, at the same time widening that between themselves and the smaller states. It was his opinion that these second-order powers would in future play the balancing role, and that homeostasis in the inter-national system was a realisable goal.

In the same year O'Sullivan critically reassessed the domino theory.[27] Declaring himself to be 'antidomino' he concluded that, like core versus periphery, it was a gross oversimplification of the historical process. Its basic assumption was that nations were life-less entities which automatically fell in one direction or another when subjected to external pressure. All the evidence of recent years demonstrated that this was manifestly not the case. Although it had its disadvantages, he found the concept of linkage a more satisfactory one. This stressed the individual character of each international relationship and the need for greater flexibility in the response to particular situations. It was based on the replacement of 'one dimensional' by 'two dimensional' explanations.

Much of the geopolitical thinking which has been outlined in this chapter does, indeed, represent a marked break with the past in the subject. It is also characterised by a certain urgency arising from the sense that time may be running out for the solution of the world's problems, many of which have actually got worse since the hopeful days of the 1960s. Indeed, in a world finite in space and in physical resources, and with humanity still largely confined to the thin enveloping film of its biosphere, only the dangers and problems appear to have been growing. The thinking which has taken place in this context has been characterised by a number of special features. These include the adaptation of Hegelian dialec-tics, the assumption of an *engagé* attitude with a Marxian flavour, a holistic and developmental approach, the investigation of 'possible and potential future worlds' and a belief in the freedom of the human will to make decisions among the possible choices.

The effects of these attitudes on the geopolitical world view have been considerable. What Taylor dismissed as 'homage to Mackinder' has been superseded by new perspectives owing more to Marx, Lenin and Wallerstein. The most fundamental consequence of this was that for the first time in the present century the dichotomy of North and South has taken precedence over that of East and West. That latitudinal fixation which many American political geographers of the 1940s bemoaned as being so embedded into the nation's geographical psychology was now overtaken by an unfamiliar and socially challenging longitudinal perspective. This new 'mappa mundi' was by no means an encouraging one since it revealed a bleak picture of growing poverty and deprivation arising both from the inadequacies of the physical environment and from what Abdel-Malek called the 'structuralist-functionalist hegemonic ideology' which has pervaded the political and economic establishments of the West. If the Third World's problems were to be tackled successfully a better global order, founded in a new geographical psychology, was essential to replace the prevailing neo-colonialism. Blaut, Abdel-Malek and others stressed the need for the inculcation of entirely new attitudes if the rich were to be made to accept a more equitable apportioning of the world's wealth.

The other development of significance was the replacement of the bipolar world by a multipolar one which was seen as having the capacity for either greater stability or greater instability depending on the ease with which the great powers were able to adapt to the situation. As a consequence of their overwhelming military might, it was they, and especially the two superpowers, who had the most significant choice of all, what Brunn called 'gardens of Eden or Armageddons'. The best-case scenario was that, with their enormous technical and economic power, they would be able to take the world into a new era of peace and prosperity. The worst-case scenario, on the other hand, was of further nuclear proliferation, leading to Mutually Assured Destruction (MAD), the 'logic of exterminism' in E.P. Thompson's words.

Since the 1970s there appear to have been two schools of thought in geopolitics for the resolution of the 'package' of interrelated world problems. These can be described broadly as being respectively revolutionary and evolutionary in their approaches.

The main protagonists of the former are generally sceptical that existing structures, with their built-in tendencies to concentration and inequality, and often sustained by attitudes deriving from the imperial past, possess the capacity for really fundamental change. They seek a new critical paradigm to express the necessities of the time, and in particular to provide the conceptual background to facilitate massive global development. The evolutionists, on the other hand, sense that fruitful change is possible within the liberal-democratic order and that shifts of power and the distribution of wealth could be expected to take place.

Underlying the new approaches to the world's problems, not only in geography but in all the social sciences, there has also been a sustained advocacy of the greater efficacy of smaller units of organisation. This has been most eloquently expressed in Schumacher's 'small is beautiful' and, with an increasing disposition to accept this, there has grown a corresponding suspicion of larger units whether they be firms, organisations, cities or blocks of flats. Geopolitically this is expressed as suspicion of large territorial units and agglomerations of power. There has been a growing sense that they are far from being ideal agents for furthering the interests of their people or of the world in general. 'There seems to be a distinct political and social antipathy towards largeness,' said O'Sullivan, and Strassoldo's power-mad but naked emperor cut a very poor figure. Thus the superpowers, multinational groupings, TNCs and world organisations have come to be viewed with considerable apprehension and even distaste. At the other end of the scale, the small units have certainly come to be considered as 'beautiful', and small nations and regions, *pays* and *Länder*, have become objects of considerable affection to academic and layman alike. They are thought of as being altogether nicer and more friendly territorial units, built to a human scale and more capable of satisfying the wants and even spiritual longings of their people. Hence the favourable impact of the idea of a 'Europe of regions' made up of colourful and individual landscapes and people who are bound to them in a *vidalien* sense rather than the somewhat menacing thoughts of 'faceless bureaucrats' presiding over a Europe in course of becoming the third or fourth superpower.[28]

Western geopolitical thinking of this nature has been taking place in a world subject to the strains of constant change. The humiliating end of the Vietnam War, the oil crisis and the economic recession of the middle 1970s had the effect of considerably diminishing the prestige and power of the West. New centres of power began to emerge, in particular the Arab world which now had to be taken into the global equation. American interest in the Middle East grew considerably during this period and the region became a major concern of successive administrations in a way it had never really been in the past. This particularly reflected concern for oil reserves, strategic communications and the alleged Soviet threat, all of which had also preoccupied Bevin 30 years before. 'The Gulf' now joined the ranks of those magic geographical expressions which, as has been seen, have over the years caused such fear and produced such fascination.

The *détente* and fluidity of the Nixon-Kissinger period was followed by a hardening of the relations between the two superpowers during the Carter administration. This was at first produced by fears engendered by the economic crisis, by a fixation with the Middle East and by a return to that spirit of righteousness which saw America not merely as a participant in world power politics but also as leader of a moral crusade of good against evil. This championing of Western-style freedoms and human rights met with a predictably sour response from the Kremlin. Zbigniew Brzezinski, Carter's National Security Advisor, introduced the concept of 'trilateralism' in opposition to Kissinger's 'pentarchy'. This was founded on the partnership of North America, Western Europe and Japan and represented, wittingly or not, a move back towards a world of more fixed positions. This was also evident in Brzezinski's concept of the 'arc of crisis', a zone of instability stretching 'from Chittagong in Bangladesh, through Islamabad all the way to Aden'.[29] The proposed response to the dangers here was to strengthen further the 'northern tier' and to involve America more closely in the defence of the Gulf. The fall of the Shah of Iran and the coming to power of the Islamic fundamentalist Khomeini in 1979 put paid to this particular strategy but served to increase American alarm at the state of the region as a whole. The situation was exacerbated in American eyes by the Soviet intervention in Afghanistan together with signs of growing Soviet involvement in the Horn of Africa. The 'arc of crisis', also evocatively termed the 'crescent of conflict', was conceived by the Reagan administration of 1981 as stretching from Ethiopia to Afghanistan. The Soviet Union was once more seen as being behind most tendencies to destabilisation in this area. There was a sudden fall in the international temperature and relations between the superpowers in the early 1980s appeared to be plunging back into something of an ice-age. The rhetoric of moral indignation was again heard loud and clear from the White House. The Soviet Union had become 'the evil empire' and a second generation of ideological differences was used to reinforce the second and third generations of nuclear weapons and missiles. This all represented on the American side a marked break with 'coexistence' ideas and with the search for normal relations which had been such a feature of the 1960s. In place of it there was a return to the cold-war stance of the early 1950s when the Soviet Union had been regarded as a subversive and aberrant state with which no normal international intercourse was possible. The 'red amoeba' which Ambassador Bullitt had in the 1940s seen flowing out of Asia was observed again from the White House in the 1980s. A major geo-political difference from those earlier sightings was that China was now detached in the American mind from the Soviet Union and so the danger emanated only from the northern part of the Asiatic Heartland. Following the death of Mao in 1976 China had moved rapidly away from his form of doctrinaire Marxism, and relations with the West had been further ameliorated. The British government which came to office in 1979 followed closely the American line over the Soviet Union and the 'Iron Lady' rhetoric reinforced that of the President.

The two Anglo-Saxon countries were thus bent on hardening the international position of the West after it was thought to have slipped badly during the 1970s. The other European countries, on the other hand, maintained a far less hostile stance in regard to the Soviet Union. The facts of geographical propinquity meant that, whatever their political views, they realised that they had to coexist on the same continent as the Russians. Their approach remained a far more pragmatic one, and they were less willing in their foreign policies to accept the truth of the stark transcontinental view. West Germany in particular kept to the tradition of Brandt's *Ostpolitik* and maintained its position as a link with the Eastern bloc. Never-theless, both France and the Federal Republic remained com-mitted to a strong Western defence and in favour of the stationing of American forces and weapon systems in Europe.

It is evident from all this that the main themes of geopolitical thought which have been discussed in this chapter have little in common with the features of the international climate outlined here. This latter had moved back to an emphasis on confrontation, strength and armaments, while the tenor of most geopolitical thought was decentralist, humanist and suspicious of the exercise of power. It was also a rebellion against the conventional and accepted Western positions, which of course included East-West confrontation, and in favour of radical changes in the attitudes of the Western leadership towards the world and its problems.

Themes such as these have, however, been much more closely reflected by internal developments within the Western countries themselves, and to a lesser extent in other areas of the world. There was, as has been observed, a marked movement in Western Europe during the 1970s towards regionalism, and many non-state nations strengthened their positions considerably within new devolutionary political frameworks.[30] Minority languages and cultures once more began to flourish and aid was channelled into regional development. This geographical expression of the 'small is beautiful' theme has resulted in real power beginning to move away from the traditional decision-making centres. Within the European Community itself the tendency has been for internal power to begin to move down to lower levels while wider Community matters are dealt with at the supranational level.[31] All over Western Europe the states which have for centuries shone out polychromatically as the most significant units on the political map of Europe have come to be called seriously into question, and new and more relevant structures have been proposed. In North America regionalist and minority aspirations have also surfaced, and have considerably shaken the established political structures. Within the Soviet bloc, and particularly in the East European countries, a similar ferment, although normally at a considerably lower temperature, has also been taking place. This intra-structural fluidity during the 1970s and 1980s contrasts markedly with the hardening of the shell between the Western and Eastern worlds. The relationship between the intra-structural and inter-structural matters is, nevertheless, a close one since internal changes in free societies must inevitably result in a re-examination of international positions. This linkage has been made by groups in the West concerning themselves with such questions as nuclear disarmament, conservation, aid to the poor world, devolution and minority rights. These questions and the proposed solutions to them had by the 1980s taken on the appearance of a sort of collective alternative view to the conventional wisdom, bringing pressure to bear on the leaderships for a change of course. As has been seen, contemporary Western geopolitical thought has tended to range itself alongside this search for a 'better way' to deal with the increasingly menacing problems of the world.

Despite the vast scale of the problems and the diversity of solutions proposed, one can detect in the new geopolitics a fundamental optimism about humanity's future. More often than not it does not arise directly from the nature of the arguments presented or from a blandness about the sheer size of the problem. Rather it appears to be founded on a belief in the willingness of humanity to rise above its differences, whether these be physical, ideological, political or economic, and to use free will in order to make positive decisions for the fate of the planet which is, in the end, the only home which its inhabitants know or possess.

Notes

1. M.A. Busteed (ed.), *Developments in Political Geography* (Academic Press, London, 1983).
2. D. Ley and M.S. Samuels (eds.), *Humanistic Geography: Prospects and Problems* (Croom Helm, London, 1978).
3. R. Peet (ed.), *Radical Geography* (Methuen, London, 1978).
4. D. Ley and M.S. Samuels, 'Contexts of Modern Humanism in Geography' in *Humanistic Geography*.
5. D. Harvey, 'The Geography of Capitalist Accumulation: A Reconstruction of Marxian Theory' in R. Peet, *Radical Geography*.
6. P. Kropotkin, 'Decentralisation, Integration of Labour and Human Education in R. Peet, *Radical Geography* (Methuen, London, 1978).
7. E. Reclus, 'The Influence of Man on the Beauty of the Earth' in R. Peet, *Radical Geography*.
8. M. Quaini, *Geography and Marxism* (Blackwell, Oxford, 1982).
9. J.P. Ferrier, J.B. Racine and C. Raffestin, 'Vers un paradigme critique: matériaux pour un projet géographique', *L'Espace Géographique*, V, 3 (1978).
10. I. Wallerstein, *The Capitalist World Economy* (Cambridge University Press, Cambridge, 1979).
11. P.J. Taylor, 'Political Geography and the World Economy' in A.D. Burnett and P.J. Taylor (ed.), *Political Studies from Spatial Perspectives* (Wiley, Chicester, 1981).
12. G. Modelski, 'The Long Cycle of Global Politics and the Nation State', *Comparative Studies in History and Sociology*, 20 (1978).
13. J. Gottmann (ed.), *Centre and Periphery: Spatial Variation in Politics* (Sage, London, 1980).
14. R. Strassoldo, 'Centre-periphery and System Boundary: Culturological Perspectives' in J. Gottmann (ed.), *Centre and Periphery*.
15. P. Claval, 'Centre/Periphery and Space: Models of Political Geography' in J. Gottmann (ed.), *Centre and Periphery*.
16. C. Raffestin, *Pour une géographie du pouvoir* (Librairies Techniques, Paris, 1980).

17. A.K. Henrikson, 'America's Changing Place in the World: from Periphery to Centre?' in J. Gottmann (ed.), *Centre and Periphery*.

18. A. Abdel-Malek, 'Geopolitics and National Movements: An Essay on the Dialectics of Imperialism' in R. Peet (ed.), *Radical Geography*.

19. S.D. Brunn, 'Geopolitics in a Shrinking World: a Political Geography of the Twenty-first century' in A.D. Burnett and P.J. Taylor (eds.), *Political Studies from Spatial Perspectives*.

20. M.I. Glassner and H.J. de Blij, *Systematic Political Geography*, 3rd edn (Wiley, New York, 1980).

21. C. Raffestin, *Pour une géographie du pouvoir*.

22. J.R. Short, *An Introduction to Political Geography* (Routledge and Kegan Paul, London, 1982).

23. J.M. Blaut, 'The Theory of Development' in R. Peet (ed.), *Radical Geography*.

24. W. Brandt (chairman), *North-South: A Programme for Survival*, report of Independent Commission on International Development Issues, (London, 1980).

25. S.B. Cohen, *Geography and Politics in a Divided World* (Methuen, London, 1964).

26. S.B. Cohen, 'A New Map of Global Geopolitical Equilibrium — A Developmental Approach', *Political Geography Quarterly*, I, 3 (1982).

27. P. O'Sullivan, 'Antidomino', *Political Geography Quarterly*, I, 3 (1982).

28. G. Parker, *A Political Geography of Community Europe*, (Butterworth, London, 1983) Chapter 9.

29. J. Reston, 'The World according to Brzezinski', *New York Times*, 31 December 1978.

30. Y. Fouéré, *Towards a Federal Europe* (Christopher Davis, Swansea, 1980).

31. G. Parker, *A Political Geography of Community Europe*, Chapter 9.

11 NOT GLASS BUT DIAMOND: A CONCLUDING ASSESSMENT

'Politics is harder than physics' said Einstein, commenting on the enormous number of variables which need to be taken into account and the consequent difficulty of formulating explanatory principles, let alone operational theories. The great variety of interpretations of the world scene which have been examined is testimony to the fact that geopolitics is in a similar category. The difficulties have been compounded by the constant change which has taken place over a period of time in the subject-matter itself. For instance, since the beginning of the century there have been considerable changes in world population, levels of industrialisation, trade patterns, raw material availability, technical accomplishment and aggregate wealth. This constantly altering scene has added considerably to the problems of interpretation. Yet, despite this, there have been elements of continuity in the overall Western geopolitical world view.

The most basic of these is that the world has been seen as a closed and finite entity, the elements of which are mutually interdependent. Since the smaller units cannot be understood independently of the whole, it is thus the world itself which is considered to be the most meaningful unit of study. There is also the belief that it is possible, as it is in the natural world, to detect recurring patterns and processes. The whole is thus seen as being rational rather than random and, as Cohen put it: 'It can be likened to a diamond, not a piece of glass.'[1] Following from this there has been an examination of repetitive patterns, attempts at explanation of them and, finally, generalisation through the postulation of explanatory theories. This nomothetic objective has been rejected by many, including Mackinder, as being inappropriate to an observational as opposed to an experimental discipline. Nevertheless, the finding of theories and even 'laws' has itself been a recurrent feature ever since the Heartland theory.

While meaning and unity have been observed in the world geopolitical scene, it nevertheless remains very much a 'world divided' and within this division lies instability, conflict and the very real possibility of catastrophe. It is a world of confrontation rather than co-operation and this has been seen to have its roots in the physical character of the world itself with all its variety and inequality. This is the geographical basis of the desire to achieve, maintain and extend power.

The study of process and pattern implies a diachronic analysis and an acceptance that it is not possible fully to understand the situation at any one time unless there is also an attempt to comprehend the spatial dynamics which have produced it. A space-time relationship is thus implicit in most geopolitical thinking, but the diachronic method has also paved the way for a form of conditional determinism. This determinism has arisen from the idea of world processes which inexorably work towards the formation of new spatial patterns. It has been tempered in most cases by the belief that human free will itself also constitutes a part of the process. This is because, since the social process can only take place through human agency, it follows that what may seem to be inevitable may in fact be avoided through the exercise of the will. This puts man into the driving scat, and although incvitably highly constrained by the 'reality' which surrounds and supports him, human needs and ideas can be injected into the process. Even in *Geopolitik*, the most determinist of the geopolitical schools, activation is deemed to take place through a leader who generates the drive for the collective triumph of the will.

This mainstream of diachronic analysis with its search for process and pattern and its conditional determinism also allows for speculation about the future. The obligation to investigate possible or potential future worlds has always been either implicitly or explicitly accepted. From the need to avoid certain unwelcome scenarios, such as national defeat, and encouragement towards more acceptable ones, such as the promotion of national well-being, has grown a strong prescriptive element which is to be found more in certain writers than in others. Most of the geopolitical thinkers of this century have, in greater or lesser degree, been *engagé*, and this has normally been directed towards the particular interests of certain geographical areas. The most common feature of this partisanship during the first three quarters of the century was that it was Western-oriented. The 'West', centring on Europe and the United States, was implicitly considered as representing progress, enlightenment, civilisation and freedom. It was seen as constituting the avant-garde of humanity in contrast to cultural and economic variants of Kipling's 'dark Egyptian night' which by implication was considered to extend over most of the rest of the world.

The *engagé* aspect of geopolitical thought brings us to the relationship of geopolitical thinkers to the political élites of their various countries. During the present century there have usually been links between academic thinkers and practical men of affairs. Such links have varied from being in some cases very close, to others in which they have been extremely tenuous. On a number of occasions political geographers have themselves actually held high political or administrative office, and certain other political geographers have been well known to statesmen. In such cases they have quite clearly had an influence on one another's ideas through such things as membership of particular political parties, societies, dining clubs and pressure groups. It is more difficult to be precise about the degree to which geopolitical thinkers have actually been influential in the development of policy, except, of course, in those few instances where the geopolitician and the statesman have been one and the same person. It has also been established that a number of the most influential Western statesmen have themselves had well developed geopolitical world views and that these have underlain their political and international actions. Such statesmen have included Theodore and Franklin Roosevelt, Curzon, Briand, Churchill, de Gaulle, Bevin, Kissinger and Nixon. All were also actively engaged in the promotion of what they regarded as being the best interests of their particular countries.

The elements of continuity which have been referred to have given at least a certain constancy to the tones and colours of the broad canvas. However, when it has come to the actual interpretation of the meaning of the picture itself, a number of quite different *Weltanschauungen* have emerged. These may be grouped, for the sake of clarity, into six major schools of thought, these being termed the binary, marginal, zonal, pluralist, idealist and centre-periphery schools (Figure 11.1). While they are far from being mutually exclusive or strictly chronological, each has had much greater appeal at certain places and periods than at others.

The binarists see the world as being divided between two great centres of power. These are in most features dissimilar and they maintain an almost permanent confrontational stance towards one another. Mackinder was the most famous exponent of this idea, and the Heartland perhaps its most evocative concept, but it has had many variants and has remained a powerful explanatory

Figure 11.1: Schools of Geopolitical Thought

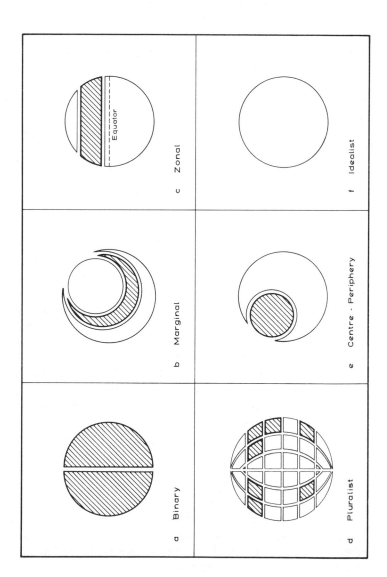

theory right to the present day. It had been opposed from the very beginning by the marginalists who identified the real centre of world power in a rim around the Eurasian landmass. Here the great civilisations of the world were located and here lay the major clusters of population, the lands with agricultural potential and areas of industrial activity. Both the continental and maritime regions of the world are fringes into which this marginally-based power needs to expand in order to add to its strength. Thus the great world conflicts take place among the marginal powers themselves for control of these areas.

In contrast to this the protagonists of the zonalist school put the major centres of world power in a great swathe through mid-latitudes, roughly from 30° to 60° North. These Northern Hemisphere chauvinists had the advantage over the marginalists in that they included North America and the interior of the Soviet Union, this giving them in many ways a more realistic position in late twentieth-century terms. Closely related to this was the pluralist school which also recognised the reality that the major centres of world power were located firmly in the Northern Hemisphere. However, according to the pluralists, the pentarchy of the United States, Western Europe, the Soviet Union, China and Japan could be joined by others, possibly in the Southern Hemisphere. A more satisfactory balance could result from this diffusion of power, and this in turn could lead to a more stable state of geopolitical equilibrium.

The idealists have been, for the most part, prescriptive rather than analytical. To them the political was one of the few aspects of human activity which had not been brought into line with the pattern of interrelationships within the closed planet. Since these interrelationships were steadily becoming more manifest, it was a matter of urgency that a world order should be established to replace the present inherited disorder.

Finally there is the school which subscribes to centre-versus-periphery ideas. Most of the geopolitical thought up to the 1970s had accepted implicitly the hegemonial position of the West. Modern centre-periphery analysis has exposed the true domination which has for so long underlain the dissemination of Western ideas of progress and civilisation. The centre, or core, is generally thought of as being in and around the North Atlantic basin and the periphery consists of most of the remainder of the world. The massive disparities between the two have been highlighted in the evocative concept of 'North-South' as being the modern world's most crucial divide.

These six schools of thought have been in evidence at various times throughout the century in what could appear at first to have been a fairly random manner. However, a closer look will reveal three quite distinct periods during which particular ideas have been especially favoured. Until World War I the bias was strongly towards the binary, while from then until the end of World War II it was mostly marginal and zonalist. Since then all, with the exception of marginalism, have occasionally surfaced, but in this period binary and pluralist ideas have aroused most discussion and contention. Since there has clearly been a definite tendency for particular ideas to find most favour at certain periods, the question arises of the extent to which they may therefore be no more than reflections of the *Zeitgeist* or even attempts to generalise from what is essentially an ephemeral and rapidly changing world scene. As has been observed, geopolitical thinking takes place against a changing world background which it is at the same time endeavouring to interpret. It has been shown that Mackinder's 1904 scenario was particularly appropriate at the beginning of the century, but became far less so within a few years, by which time world circumstances had considerably altered. Similarly idealism emerged in the aftermath of both world wars and held sway for two relatively brief periods during which there was some real hope that a new order of things might be created. Likewise, contemporary thinking which is based on the centre versus periphery idea is permeated with criticism and even condemnation of the West just at the time when this occidocentric world order has come under strong and sustained threat from both internal and external sources. Despite such very clear indications of the close relationship between the thinking and the times when it was taking place, three features stand out in the thinking of most of the century.

The first of these is that there is an underlying sense of conflict of one sort or another. The manifestation of power in one area of the closed planet with its finite space and physical resources is met with countervailing force elsewhere. It is the selfishness of man in regard to the potentialities of his supporting environment which comes out as being the central cause of such conflict. The second is that the binary view underlies most of the other views in one way or another. 'Two' is more prevalent than 'three' or 'four', and even when, as in Cohen, there are four, these are then divided into two groups. Thirdly there is the persistence of the hegemonic model of a world centre and a world edge, an inside and an outside, with the world order designed for the promotion of the interests of the dominant geographical area.

Each of these three characteristics has kept recurring during radically changing circumstances. Through these, together with certain subsidiary ideas, the nomothetic objective could be extended to encompass the whole canon of thought. It is, however, the purpose of this book to review geopolitical ideas rather than attempt to synthesise existing theories into more general ones, although such a synthesis would be quite possible. The hypothetical value of the construction of such a general geopolitical theory presupposes relative constancy, or at least a slow and controlled change, within the existing system. However, another view of the social process is that the pressures for change periodically become so great that they can no longer be contained within the existing world system. It then becomes necessary for this to be replaced by an entirely new one, adapted to changed circumstances. If perceptual change is accompanied by conceptual change, then a new paradigm comes into being. This is what Kuhn called 'paradigm shift'[2] and Henrikson saw as being a 'Copernican Revolution'.[3] Although reactivated in the aftermath of the oil crisis, this mode of thought has in fact a much longer lineage. Semple had talked in a similar manner of turning points in world history and of the necessity for the geographer to be prepared for 'a momentous readjustment' of his thinking at certain times.

In the early part of the present century it was quite usual to consider and explain the works of man through the use of organic analogies, hence the prevalence in the earlier geopolitical works of such terms as 'organic', 'natural' and 'evolution'. Just as physical organisms evolved and attained greater sophistication, so it was anticipated that social organisms could be expected to do much the same. This was part of the philosophical underpinning of the Victorian belief in progress which was to be so rudely shattered by World War I. This catastrophe was followed by a division between those who wished to return to the safety of the nineteenth century and those who saw the necessity for a fundamental re-evaluation. The former were the protagonists of *Geopolitik*, while the latter provided the dominant ideas in the British and French schools. The emphasis in these two was on free will and the ability of man to maintain control over nature. The analogies here tended towards the mechanical and architectonic, based on human, rather than on natural, creation. After World War II there was once more change, and the positivist influence became considerable. Quantification and model building were intended to introduce a new precision into all geographical study, although this had only a marginal impact on geopolitical thought itself. The application of systems theory to the international scene was to prove more influential. The further major change which began in the 1970s was the humanist one of bringing man the human being, as opposed to mankind the abstraction, back into the centre of the stage.

Each of these four sequential paradigms, underlying the geopolitical perceptions of the world, have derived from wider philosophical systems to which credence was given at particular times. Each can be seen to have arisen in dialectical reaction to the inadequacies which had become apparent in the previous one. Thus the organic concept which had been so influential and attractive in the Victorian period was converted into a recipe for the decline of Europe, and in particular of Britain, after World War I. This now doom-laden paradigm was quickly supplanted by a new one based upon the autonomous position of man rather than the inexorable power of nature. Relationships of a similar sort can be detected underlying the other paradigm shifts which took place later on in the century. When considered in this way, the major function of a geopolitical paradigm appears as only partly explanatory of the nature of the world. It can serve also as both a justification and a prescription for what are perceived as being the best interests of a particular section of the earth's space. The exact nature of the paradigm will therefore also depend upon the definition of 'best interests' at any particular time, though these will, of course, tend to be refined and implemented by the élites involved.

Great changes such as those envisaged in Kuhn's 'paradigm shifts' and Semple's 'momentous readjustments' are likely to take place with some rapidity. This view of history eschews gradual evolution within a relatively constant framework for dramatic 'scene changes' in which new props are introduced and the old ones are shifted to new positions. In the terminology of natural science, it is thus saltationist rather than gradualist, and the theory of catastrophism is likely to be more appropriate in its explanation than that of evolution. Catastrophic changes, such as war, pandemics, depressions, mass migrations and genocide, have all been very much a part of the fabric of international affairs during the present century. Yet only rarely have they been subjects of explicit geo-political investigation.

The great change which influenced geopolitical thinking in the 1970s was, as has been observed, radically humanist in motivation. Hegelian dialectics became part of the methodology for the explanation of spatial pattern and process, but the spirit of the new humanism looks back, via Kropotkin and Reclus, to Goethe and the eighteenth-century sense of balance and harmony. It has many strands, including the Marxian, but fundamental to them all is the Renaissance position that man is the measure of all things. Ideologies, organisations and systems are therefore never to be regarded as being above and independent of that humanity which brought them into being in the first place. Inherent in it also is a strong reassertion of terrestrial unity, what Malin called 'a whole-ness of view about human culture'. Allied to this, and with par-ticularly important implications in geopolitical thinking, has been the growing mistrust of the large and anonymous and a desire to get back to units on a more human scale. The great prophet of this was E.F. Schumacher whose *Small is Beautiful*[4] published in 1973 was to become highly influential in pointing to alternatives to the conventional wisdoms of the time. An important geopolitical manifestation of such ideas has been a new concern with smaller territorial units. The effectiveness of small nations and regions in securing human well-being has been contrasted with the problems experienced by imperial states and large international organisa-tions.[5] There has also been a new attitude to the dominant paradigm and in line with Popper's theory of the provisionality of knowledge[6] a disposition to question its legitimacy. This has intro-duced a new sense of freedom from what Michell termed 'the dominant myth'[7] and a humanist predisposition to create a world system in the best interests of all its inhabitants.

While the new thinking looks to symbiosis rather than struggle as its leitmotiv, this is by no means new to geopolitical thought. It is very much in the lineage of those idealists who have in the past sought to overturn the conventional assumptions about *Real-politik*, and to replace them with a world built on higher principles. It remains to be seen whether it will be possible to bring about a fundamental change to that 'real world' which has in the past proved such a stumbling block to the idealists. One might take comfort from Boggs who, as long ago as 1941, observed that the very instruments which had been used for brutality could be adapted to serve humanitarian objectives.[8]

Clearly there has been considerable unity and also diversity in the geopolitical thought of this century. An attempt has been made here to examine it as a totality and to assess its relevance to our own times. True knowledge, according to Heisenberg, speaking of his uncertainty principle, cannot be obtained from the observation of isolated phenomena. It is necessary to recognise that the wealth of experiential facts is interconnected and can therefore be reduced to what he called a 'common principle'. To him it followed on from this that 'certainty rests precisely on this wealth of facts. The danger of making mistakes is the smaller the richer and more complex the phenomena are'.[9]

The phenomena studied by geopolitical thinkers have indeed been extremely varied and the widest interconnections have been investigated. This vast subject matter only achieves coherence through a rigorous application of the spatial viewpoint. With a task of such magnitude, Muir reached the opinion that '[no] mind can comprehend all the significant interactions taking place in the world'.[10] With such a wealth of material it has been difficult to attain anything like the certainty of which Heisenberg spoke, or to perceive readily a 'common principle' underlying it all. Yet, by the same token, understanding could in the end prove more durable as a consequence of these very difficulties.

There is also another aspect to it which goes beyond explanations and theories. Obtaining a true picture of the world also entails the wider relationship between the investigator and his subject matter. This is what Einstein termed *Einfühlung*, the intellectual love of the objects of experience, and to him this was the real motive behind all scientific enquiry. In his first article on political geography Mackinder had justified his ideas as being 'the building of palaces out of the bricks'. Perhaps in the end this has to be the ultimate and most rewarding justification for all geopolitical thought.

Notes

1. S.B. Cohen, *Geography and Politics in a Divided World* (Methuen, London, 1964).

2. T.S. Kuhn, *The Structure of Scientific Revolutions* (University of Chicago Press, Chicago, 1962).

3. A.K. Henrikson, 'America's Changing Place in the World: from Periphery to Centre?' in J. Gottmann, *Centre and Periphery* (Sage, London, 1980).

4. E.F. Schumacher, *Small is Beautiful: Economics as if People Mattered* (Blond and Briggs, London, 1973).

5. L. Kohr, *The Breakdown of Nations* (Routledge and Kegan Paul, London, 1957).

6. K. Popper, *The Logic of Scientific Discovery* (Hutchinson, London, 1959).

7. J. Michell, 'The Ideal World-View' in S. Kumar (ed.), *The Schumacher Lectures* (Blond and Briggs, London, 1980).

8. S.W. Boggs, 'Mapping the Changing World: Suggested Developments in Maps', *Annals of the Association of American Geographers*, 31 (1941).

9. W.C. Heisenberg, *Physics and Beyond* (Allen and Unwin, London, 1971).

10. R. Muir, *Modern Political Geography* (Macmillan, London, 1975).

GLOSSARY OF GEOPOLITICAL TERMS

A number of these terms are known and used in other disciplines. They are defined and employed here in their geopolitical context.

Anschluss The union of Austria with Nazi Germany following the German invasion of Austria in March 1938.

Arctic Mediterranean Term used by a number of political geographers at the time of World War II both to suggest that the Arctic Ocean was 'mediterranean' in relation to Eurasia and North America and to predict that it might be the sea of the future.

Blitzkrieg 'Lightning war' based on the theory of the best use of tanks and other armour in land warfare. It was put into practice by the Germans in World War II and produced an astonishing series of victories from 1939 to 1941.

Cold war The situation of confrontation and antipathy between the Western and the communist blocs which has been a feature of their relations since the end of World War II. It is especially associated with the exceptionally bleak period between the proclamation of the Truman Doctrine in 1947 and the death of Stalin in 1953.

Conditio Germaniae An adaptation of the original term *Conditio Preussen*, which was used for the fate of Prussia to be located in the heart of Europe and surrounded by often hostile great powers. This had necessitated the adoption of ruthless measures in order to ensure the survival of the state. It was a condition which was seen by some as having been transferred to the German Empire in the late nineteenth century.

Containment Strategy adopted by the United States in the 1950s in its relations with the Soviet Union. It was associated particularly with the ideas of George Kennan and became a feature of the cold war (q.v.). Through the building up of military alliances it was hoped to prevent the territorial expansion of the Soviets and the extension of their ideas.

Cordon sanitaire A zone around the frontiers of a state set up to prevent or discourage its further expansion, or a zone between two states designed to keep them apart. Such a zone is usually made up of a number of small states which themselves have a vested interest in the maintenance of peace and which are encouraged to maintain a neutralist or independent stance.

Core area The nucleus or central area of the state. It is necessary to distinguish the historic core, from which the state originally emerged, from the contemporary core, which is likely to contain its political, economic and cultural heartland. The two could coincide territorially, but in many cases they are quite distinct.

Crush zone Term used by Fairgrieve for the lands around the edges of the Heartland (q.v.). In his view the most important of them were Eastern Europe, the Near East and the maritime parts of China. See also Inner Crescent.

Domino theory The notion that the Soviet subjection of one country would inevitably be followed by an attempt to subjugate those others next in line. In this way countries around the Soviet Union would fall like dominoes unless supported by the power of the United States. Associated with the strategy of containment (q.v.).

Drang nach dem Suden The German longing or yearning for the south.

Drang nach Osten The historic German desire for eastward expansion. It had economic, political, military and ethnic aspects.

Ecumene Term used by Derwent Whittlesey for the populated parts of a country or landmass. It is contrasted with the parts which, as a consequence of their unfavourable physical conditions, are not able to support more than very limited numbers.

Festung Europa Fortress Europe. With the turning of the tide in World War II, German-occupied Europe began to come under considerable attack from the east, south and west. The Nazi concept of an embattled European fortress was intended to give strength and purpose to the defence. Among its manifestations were the *Westwall* (Atlantic Wall), and later the idea of an Alpine redoubt.

Great Game The nineteenth-century confrontation of the British and Russian Empires in Asia. Each became highly suspicious of the manoeuvrings of the other power in those Central Asian buffer areas located in between their respective spheres of influence.

Grosslebensformen Used in German *Geopolitik* for the formation of large political units by the process of *Grossraumwirtschaft* (q.v.).

Grossraum Used in German *Geopolitik* to describe territorial units larger than states which were considered as being the next stage in world geopolitical development.

Grossraumwirtschaft Term used in German *Geopolitik* to describe the process of the formation of territorial units larger than states. They were considered as being the next stage in world geopolitical development.

Heartland Term used by Halford Mackinder in 1919. In his world view, it was similar in significance to the Pivot (q.v.). Although covering a very similar region to the latter, it was considerably larger and significantly included the whole of the eastern part of Europe.

Herrenvolk The idea, particularly favoured by the Nazis, that the Germans were a master race and thus superior to all except the other 'Aryans'. This was seen as making the Germans the natural leaders of Europe, while 'inferior' races, such as the Jews and the Slavs, would thus occupy a lowly position in the New Order (q.v.).

Inner Crescent Term used by Halford Mackinder for the lands around the edges of the Heartland (q.v.). They included continental Europe, the Middle East, the Indian subcontinent and China. See also Rimland.

Iron Curtain That great fortified line extending from north to south across Europe which since World War II has separated the Western from the Soviet spheres and has divided the continent into two mutually hostile camps. The phrase was made famous by Winston Churchill in 1946, but it had previously been used by Joseph Goebbels and by Count Schwerin von Krosig.

Italia Irredenta 'Unredeemed Italy'. A term used by Italian nationalists, including the Fascists, for what they considered to be the historic lands of Italy. They were of the opinion, particularly after World War I, that many of these lands had been denied to them. The writer Gabriele d'Annunzio, a prominent nationalist, worked for the territorial completion of Italy in this way.

Kleinstaatengerümpel 'A rubbish of small states'. Term used by the Nazis to refer to the proliferation of small states which had come into being in Eastern Europe after World War I. They considered it to be Germany's destiny to sweep these away, and to replace them with a German-dominated European order. See

New Order.

Kulturboden Term used in German *Geopolitik* for that area in which German civilisation (*Kultur*) was considered to be dominant.

Lebensraum Literally 'living space'. Used particularly in German *Geopolitik* to indicate the territory which it was considered Germany required in order to support her growing population adequately.

Lenaland Term used by Halford Mackinder for that part of northern Siberia east of the Yenisei river which in 1943 he excluded from the Heartland (q.v.).

Limites naturelles The French geographical concept of natural frontiers. According to this, the French 'hexagon' fitted naturally into its physical environment and so, in this sense at least, could be explained deterministically. The idea had been current since the seventeenth century when it was used to justify the extension of France to the Rhine. In recent times it has been criticised by many French geographers both for its inflexibility and for ignoring the dynamic relationship between man and his environment.

Mainland Term used by C.B. Fawcett for what Halford Mackinder named the World Island (q.v.).

Manometer Literally a gauge for measuring the pressure of gases. Used in German *Geopolitik* to refer to those characteristics which were considered to indicate the real strength possessed by any state.

Mare Nostrum 'Our sea'. Term used by the Romans for the Mediterranean Sea in order to indicate their sense of possession. In the 1920s the term was resurrected by the Italian Fascists, and came to be associated with their aspiration to achieve a similar commanding position for modern Italy.

Middle Tier Term used by Halford Mackinder and others to describe the group of small states located between the Baltic, the Mediterranean and the Black Seas. Most of them had been established, or their territories considerably added to, after World War I. See also *Teufelsgürtel* and *cordon sanitaire*.

Midland Ocean Term used by Halford Mackinder in 1943 for the North Atlantic Ocean.

Mitteleuropa Central Europe. A difficult geographical concept because, while it has quite definite boundaries to the north and south — the Baltic Sea and the Alps — the major physiographic

lines of the continent are from east to west, and so its boundaries in those directions are indeterminate. Much attention has
been given by German geographers to establishing a set of criteria for more precise delimitation. While basically a geographical concept, it was politicised when it came to be
associated with those areas in which Germany and the German
people were in a commanding position.

Musspreussen Forced Prussianisation of the other German states
associated with Prussia's increased westerly orientation after
1815. This culminated in the establishment of the German
Empire in 1871 and the attempt to introduce Prussian methods
and values.

New Order *Die Neue Ordnung* was a Nazi phrase for the new
European system which they aimed to create. It would be
organised and led by the *Herrenvolk* (q.v.) and the old system
of states would be abolished.

Ostpolitik The process of normalisation of relations with the
Eastern bloc countries initiated by the German Federal Repub-
lic in the late 1960s. It is particularly associated with former
Chancellor Willy Brandt. It was a radically new departure and
came after a quarter of a century of refusal by the West
Germans to recognise the changes which had taken place in
Eastern Europe following World War II.

Outer Crescent Term used by Halford Mackinder for the lands
lying outisde the Inner Crescent (q.v.). They were mostly insular
or peninsular in relation to the World Island (q.v.) and included
North and South America, Britain, Southern Africa and
Australasia.

Panideen A term used in German *Geopolitik* for the wider cultural characteristics and aspirations upon which pan-regions
were based.

Pays A country or region. In the particular sense used by French
geographers, it has come to mean the character of the landscape
produced by the mutual relationship of man and environment in
a particular area.

Pivot Term used by Halford Mackinder in 1904 to describe that
area in the centre of Asia having inland or Arctic drainage. It
was thus out of reach of maritime power and Mackinder saw it
as being the key geopolitical area in the contemporary world.

Raum Space in the sense of territory and all that this implies for
its ability to support population.

Raumgebundende Term used in German *Geopolitik* for those races which were not considered capable of expansion.

Raumstreben The strife or aspiration by a particular race or national group to gain additional territory (*Raum*) and in this way to promote its best interests.

Raumüberwindende Term used in German *Geopolitik* for those races which were considered capable of expanding over large areas and colonising them.

Realpolitik Political action claiming to be based on an understanding of world realities rather than upon idealistic notions. In international relations it implies the acceptance of the use of force, if necessary, in order to achieve aims.

Rimland Term used by Nicholas Spykman for those areas lying around the maritime fringes of the Heartland (q.v.). They include Europe, the Middle East, the Indian subcontinent and South-East Asia. He considered them to be culturally, politically and economically the most significant parts of the world.

Schicksalsraum 'Space of destiny'. Term used in German *Geopolitik* for the lands to the east of Germany where it was considered that the country's future lay and in which her destiny as a world power would be determined.

Shatter zone An internationally unstable region lying in between two or more areas of greater strength and stability. Some political geographers have seen such regions as being a source of danger while others have regarded their existence as being essential in order to facilitate necessary changes on the world scene.

Sprachboden The geographical area in which a particular language is spoken. Term used in German *Geopolitik* to refer to the area within which German was either the only or the major language spoken.

Teufelsgürtel 'The Devil's Belt'. A term used in German *Geopolitik* for the *cordon sanitaire* (q.v.) set up by the Allies in Eastern Europe after World War I. It was seen as being designed to hamper German expansion into, or even involvement with, the lands to the east. See also *Schicksalsraum*.

Volksboden The geographical area inhabited by a particular nation (*Volk*). Used in German *Geopolitik* to refer to the total area inhabited by the German people. See also *Sprachboden*.

Weltanschauung A philosophy or outlook on life. In the specifically geopolitical sense it is a total world view or spatial ideology.

World-Island Term used by Halfore Mackinder to describe the single landmass made up by Europe, Asia and Africa.

World-Promontory Term used by Halford Mackinder to describe the land jutting out south-westwards from the World-Island (q.v.). Unlike the northern and north-western coasts of the World-Island it is open to influences from the surrounding oceans and so has been easier for the maritime powers to control.

Zerrungszone 'Zone of friction'. Term used in German *Geopolitik* for the lands to the east of Germany after World War I which were looked upon as being unstable and dangerous to German security.

INDEX